Quick & Easy *All Stars* Block Tool

110 Quilt Blocks in 5 Sizes
with Project Ideas

Packed with Hints, Tips & Tricks

Simple Cutting Charts & Helpful Reference Tables

DEBBIE RODGERS

C&T PUBLISHING
Another Maker Inspired!

Text and artwork copyright © 2025 by Debbie Rodgers

Photography copyright © 2025 by C&T Publishing, Inc.

Publisher: Amy Barrett-Daffin

Creative Director: Gailen Runge

Senior Editor: Roxane Cerda

Editor: Madison Moore

Technical Editor: Linda Johnson

Cover/Book Designer: April Mostek

Production Coordinator: Zinnia Heinzmann

Illustrator: Debbie Rodgers

Photography Coordinator: Rachel Ackley

Photography by Gailen Runge of C&T Publishing, Inc., unless otherwise noted

Published by C&T Publishing, Inc., P.O. Box 1456, Lafayette, CA 94549

All rights reserved. No part of this work covered by the copyright hereon may be used in any form or reproduced by any means—graphic, electronic, or mechanical, including photocopying, recording, taping, or information storage and retrieval systems—without written permission from the publisher. The copyrights on individual artworks are retained by the artists as noted in *Quick & Easy All Stars Block Tool*. These designs may be used to make items for personal use only and may not be used for the purpose of personal profit. Items created to benefit nonprofit groups, or that will be publicly displayed, must be conspicuously labeled with the following credit: "Designs copyright © 2025 by Debbie Rodgers from the book *Quick & Easy All Stars Block Tool* from C&T Publishing, Inc." Permission for all other purposes must be requested in writing from C&T Publishing, Inc.

Attention Teachers: C&T Publishing, Inc., encourages the use of our books as texts for teaching. You can find lesson plans for many of our titles at ctpub.com or contact us at ctinfo@ctpub.com.

We take great care to ensure that the information included in our products is accurate and presented in good faith, but no warranty is provided, nor are results guaranteed. Having no control over the choices of materials or procedures used, neither the author nor C&T Publishing, Inc., shall have any liability to any person or entity with respect to any loss or damage caused directly or indirectly by the information contained in this book. For your convenience, we post an up-to-date listing of corrections on our website (ctpub.com). If a correction is not already noted, please contact our customer service department at ctinfo@ctpub.com or P.O. Box 1456, Lafayette, CA 94549.

Trademark (™) and registered trademark (®) names are used throughout this book. Rather than use the symbols with every occurrence of a trademark or registered trademark name, we are using the names only in the editorial fashion and to the benefit of the owner, with no intention of infringement.

Library of Congress Control Number: 2024050652

Printed in China

10 9 8 7 6 5 4 3 2 1

Contents

4	How to Use the Block Charts
5	Block Index by Name
7	Block Index by Grid
10	Precut Friendly Index
12	110 Blocks
122	Tips & Helpful Charts
122	Triangle in a Square
123	Mix and Match Blocks
123	Sewing Squares to Squares or Rectangles
123	Sewing Partial Seams
124	Corner Alignment for Piecing Shapes
124	Yardage for Squares
124	Standard Mattress Sizes
125	Yardage for Rectangles
125	Figuring Fabric for a Quilt
125	Diagonal Measurements of Blocks
126	Sewing Half-Square Triangles
126	Sewing Flying Geese with Triangles
126	Easy-Cut 45° Angles
127	Side and Corner Triangles for Diagonal Settings
127	About the Author

How to Use the Block Charts

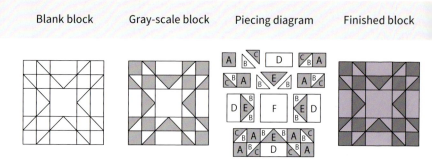

Blank block   Gray-scale block   Piecing diagram   Finished block

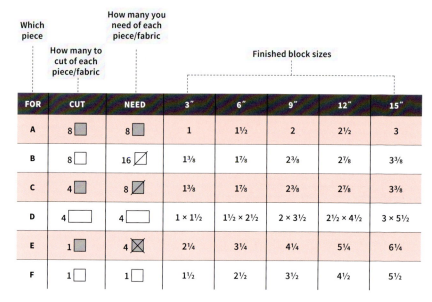

FOR	CUT	NEED	3″	6″	9″	12″	15″
A	8	8	1	1½	2	2½	3
B	8	16	1⅜	1⅞	2⅜	2⅞	3⅜
C	4	8	1⅜	1⅞	2⅜	2⅞	3⅜
D	4	4	1 × 1½	1½ × 2½	2 × 3½	2½ × 4½	3 × 5½
E	1	4	2¼	3¼	4¼	5¼	6¼
F	1	1	1½	2½	3½	4½	5½

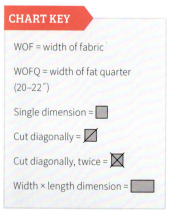

DESIGN OPTIONS

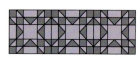

Yardage amounts are based on 42″ of usable width.

SEAM ALLOWANCES

Use ¼″-wide seam allowance throughout.

Block Index by Name

1 American Stars 2 Amish Star 3 Annie's Choice 4 Arizona Star 5 Arkansas Star 6 Arrowheads 7 Aunt Eliza's Star

8 Best Of All 9 Bethlehem Star 10 Black Diamond 11 Boxes and Baskets 12 Bright Stars 13 Broken Star 14 Christmas Star

15 Combination Star 16 Constellation 17 Contrary Wife 18 Coronation Star 19 Country Star 20 Cozy Star 21 Cross and Star

22 Crystal Star 23 Diamond Ripple 24 Diamond Star 25 Dolley Madison's Star 26 Double Pyramid 27 Double Sawtooth Star 28 Double Z

29 Eccentric Star 30 Emerald and Topaz 31 Father's Choice 32 Flying Kite 33 Formal Garden 34 Four Crowns 35 Free Trade

36 Friendship Block 37 Friendship Star 38 Green Mountain Star 39 Halley's Comet 40 Hope of Hartford 41 Illinois Star 42 Judy's Star

43 King's Crown 44 Land of Lincoln 45 Large Star 46 Lover's Lane 47 Martha Washington Star 48 Memory 49 Milky Way

50 Missouri Blossom 51 Mosaic Star 52 Mrs. Jones' Favorite 53 Nine-Patch Star 54 Noon and Light 55 North Star 56 Northumberland Star

Block Index by Name, continued

 57 Ohio Star
 58 The Original
 59 Panama Star
 60 Peacock Star
 61 Peter Paul Puzzle
 62 Pieced Star
 63 Pineapple Star

 64 Pinwheel Askew
 65 Prairie Sunrise
 66 Premium Star
 67 President's Star
 68 Priscilla's Dream
 69 Providence
 70 Queen Victoria

 71 Rainbow Star
 72 Rebel Patch
 73 Rhapsody Star
 74 Ribbon Star
 75 Rising Star
 76 Rising Sun
 77 Rocky Mountain Puzzle

 78 Rolling Star
 79 Rose Trellis
 80 Sawtooth Star
 81 Seesaw
 82 Shooting Stars
 83 Silent Star
 84 Sparkling Star

 85 Spinning Star
 86 Spring Beauty
 87 Spring Has Come
 88 Square and Star
 89 Square in Square Star
 90 Star Block
 91 Stardust

 92 Star Gardner
 93 Star of Alamo
 94 Star of Bethlehem
 95 Star of Hope
 96 Star of Many Points
 97 Star of Sedona
 98 Star of Virginia

 99 Star Pattern
 100 Stepping Stones
 101 Stockyard's Star
 102 Summer Star
 103 Sun Ray
 104 Tennessee Waltz
 105 Trailing Star

 106 Treasure Star
 107 Union Star
 108 Variable Star
 109 Wandering Star
 110 Wyoming Valley

6   Quick & Easy All Stars Block Tool

Block Index by Grid

For easy reference, the blocks in the *All Stars Quick & Easy Block Tool* are categorized by grid. Grids are based on the number of equal divisions in the side of the block. A 2-grid block equals 2 × 2 division, a 3-grid block equals 3 × 3 division, and so on.

2 GRID   3 GRID

32 Flying Kite

1 American Stars

5 Arkansas Star

7 Aunt Eliza's Star

19 Country Star

25 Dolley Madison's Star

26 Double Pyramid

28 Double Z

29 Eccentric Star

33 Formal Garden

37 Friendship Star

53 Nine-Patch Star

57 Ohio Star

59 Panama Star

63 Pineapple Star

67 President's Star

83 Silent Star

85 Spinning Star

89 Square in Square Star

95 Star of Hope

103 Sun Ray

108 Variable Star

109 Wandering Star

4 GRID *continued on next page*

3 Annie's Choice

13 Broken Star

16 Constellation

24 Diamond Star

27 Double Sawtooth Star

35 Free Trade

42 Judy's Star

44 Land of Lincoln

47 Martha Washington Star

50 Missouri Blossom

54 Noon and Light

56 Northumberland Star

4 GRID continued

62 Pieced Star

64 Pinwheel Askew

70 Queen Victoria

73 Rhapsody Star

74 Ribbon Star

75 Rising Star

77 Rocky Mountain Puzzle

79 Rose Trellis

80 Sawtooth Star

81 Seesaw

84 Sparkling Star

86 Spring Beauty

88 Square and Star

90 Star Block

91 Stardust

94 Star of Bethlehem

96 Star of Many Points

98 Star of Virginia

101 Stockyard's Star

105 Trailing Star

5 GRID

14 Christmas Star

31 Father's Choice

39 Halley's Comet

40 Hope of Hartford

52 Mrs. Jones' Favorite

69 Providence

6 GRID continued on next page

2 Amish Star

4 Arizona Star

8 Best Of All

11 Boxes and Baskets

15 Combination Star

17 Contrary Wife

22 Crystal Star

23 Diamond Ripple

30 Emerald and Topaz

34 Four Crowns

36 Friendship Block

41 Illinois Star

Quick & Easy All Stars Block Tool

6 GRID *continued*

 43 King's Crown
 45 Large Star
 46 Lover's Lane
 48 Memory
 49 Milky Way
 51 Mosaic Star

 58 The Original
 71 Rainbow Star
 72 Rebel Patch
 92 Star Gardner
 93 Star of Alamo
 97 Star of Sedona

 99 Star Pattern
 104 Tennessee Waltz
 106 Treasure Star
 107 Union Star
 110 Wyoming Valley

8 GRID

 6 Arrowheads
 9 Bethlehem Star
 10 Black Diamond
 12 Bright Stars
 18 Coronation Star
 20 Cozy Star

 21 Cross and Star
 38 Green Mountain Star
 55 North Star
 60 Peacock Star
 61 Peter Paul Puzzle
 68 Priscilla's Dream

 76 Rising Sun
 78 Rolling Star
 82 Shooting Stars
 87 Spring Has Come
 100 Stepping Stones
 102 Summer Star

9 GRID 10 GRID

 66 Premium Star
 65 Prairie Sunrise

Block Index by Grid

Precut Friendly Index

Precut Names and Sizes

Pre-cut quilter's cottons are a boon for quilters! Instead of having to buy full yardage, you can get a stack or roll of a variety of fabrics, pre-cut for you. There might be more than one name for the various sizes. Here are the common names and sizes used in this book:

FAT QUARTER
18″ × 20–22″

FQ

JELLY ROLL
2½″ × 44″

Jelly roll

Typically sold in rolls of 40 strips.

LAYER CAKE
10″ × 10″

LC

Typically sold in packs of 42 squares.

CHARM SQUARE
5″ × 5″

CS

Typically sold in packs of 40 squares.

CHARM SQUARES

7 Aunt Eliza's Star

19 Country Star

25 Dolley Madison's Star

36 Friendship Block

43 King's Crown

68 Priscilla's Dream

76 Rising Sun

88 Square and Star

LAYER CAKE

 11 Boxes and Baskets
 17 Contrary Wife
 21 Cross and Star
 32 Flying Kite
 38 Green Mountain Star
 44 Land of Lincoln

 52 Mrs. Jones' Favorite
 56 Northumberland Star
 61 Peter Paul Puzzle
 72 Rebel Patch
 79 Rose Trellis
 81 Seesaw

 87 Spring Has Come
 90 Star Block
 93 Star of Alamo
 96 Star of Many Points
 99 Star Pattern

JELLY ROLL

 4 Arizona Star
 14 Christmas Star
 39 Halley's Comet
 69 Providence
 110 Wyoming Valley

FAT QUARTERS

 3 Annie's Choice
 15 Combination Star
 28 Double Z
 59 Panama Star
 75 Rising Star
 77 Rocky Mountain Puzzle

 78 Rolling Star
 82 Shooting Stars
 86 Spring Beauty
 91 Stardust
 103 Sun Ray
 108 Variable Star

Precut Friendly Index

1 American Stars

  3-GRID

 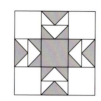 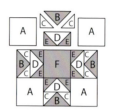 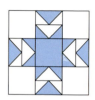

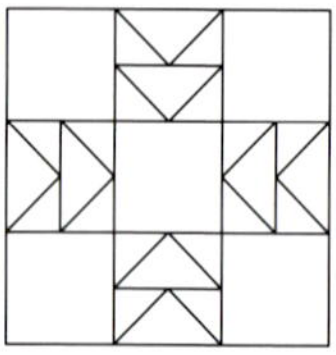

FOR	CUT	NEED	3"	6"	9"	12"	15"
A	4	4	1½	2½	3½	4½	5½
B	1	4	2¼	3¼	4¼	5¼	6¼
C	4	8	1⅜	1⅞	2⅜	2⅞	3⅜
D	1	4	2¼	3¼	4¼	5¼	6¼
E	4	8	1⅜	1⅞	2⅜	2⅞	3⅜
F	1	1	1½	2½	3½	4½	5½

DESIGN OPTIONS

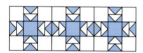

CUTTING

NOTE *Refer to Side and Corner Triangles for Diagonal Settings (page 127).*

A: Cut 2 strips 4½" × WOF; subcut into 16 squares 4½" × 4½".

B, E, and corner triangles: Cut 1 strip 9⅜" × WOF; subcut into 2 squares 9⅜" × 9⅜" (corner triangles), 4 squares 5¼" × 5¼" (B) and 2 squares 2⅞" × 2⅞" (E).

E: Cut 1 strip 2⅞" × WOF; subcut into 14 squares 2⅞" × 2⅞".

Side triangles: Cut 1 strip 18¼" × WOF; subcut into 2 squares 18¼" × 18¼".

C: Cut 2 strips 2⅞" × WOF; subcut into 16 squares 2⅞" × 2⅞".

D, F: Cut 1 strip 5¼" × WOF; subcut into 4 squares 5¼" × 5¼" (D) and 4 squares 4½" × 4½" (F).

YARDAGE FOR TABLE RUNNER

68" × 17"

12" block

4 blocks on diagonal

A: ⅜ yard

B, E, side and corner triangles: 1 yard

C, D, F: ⅜ yard

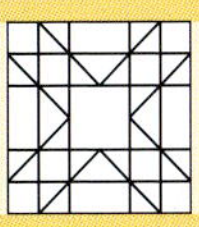

Amish Star 2

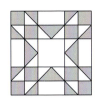
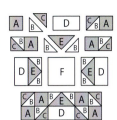
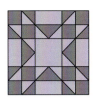

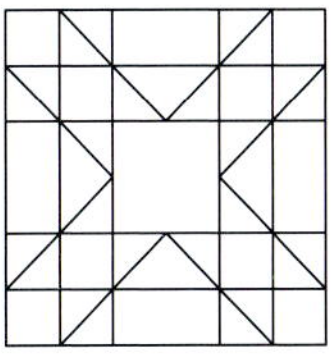

FOR	CUT	NEED	3″	6″	9″	12″	15″
A	8	8	1	1½	2	2½	3
B	8	16	1⅜	1⅞	2⅜	2⅞	3⅜
C	4	8	1⅜	1⅞	2⅜	2⅞	3⅜
D	4	4	1 × 1½	1½ × 2½	2 × 3½	2½ × 4½	3 × 5½
E	1	4	2¼	3¼	4¼	5¼	6¼
F	1	1	1½	2½	3½	4½	5½

DESIGN OPTIONS

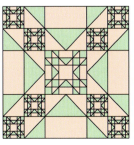

YARDAGE FOR BABY QUILT

36″ × 36″

6″ and 12″ blocks

8 × 6″ + 1 × 12″ = 9 blocks plus pieced background

A, C, E, background: 1 yard

B, D, F, background: 1 yard

CUTTING

A (6″, 12″): Cut 1 strip 2½″ × WOF; subcut into 8 squares 2½″ × 2½″ (A-12″), 8 squares 1½″ × 1½″ (A-6″).

A, 6″: Cut 2 strips 1½″ × WOF; subcut into 56 squares 1½″ × 1½″.

C, 6″, background: Cut 1 strip 6⅞″ × WOF; subcut into 4 squares 6⅞″ × 6⅞″, cut in half diagonally (background), 21 squares 1⅞″ × 1⅞″ (C).

C (6″, 12″): Cut 1 strip 2⅞″ × WOF; subcut into 4 squares 2⅞″ × 2⅞″ (C-12″), 11 squares 1⅞″ × 1⅞″ (C-6″).

E (6″, 12″), background: Cut 1 strip 13¼″ × WOF; subcut into 1 square 13¼″ × 13¼″, cut in half diagonally twice (background). From the remaining strip cut 1 square 5¼″ × 5¼″ (E-12″), 8 squares 3¼″ × 3¼″ (E-6″).

B, 6″ and 12″ blocks, background: Cut 2 strips 6⅞″ × WOF; subcut into 8 squares 6⅞″ × 6⅞″, cut in half diagonally (background), 8 squares 2⅞″ × 2⅞″ (B-12″), 24 squares 1⅞″ × 1⅞″ (B-6″).

B, 6″: Cut 2 strips 1⅞″ × WOF; subcut into 40 squares 1⅞″ × 1⅞″.

D (6″, 12″), background: Cut 2 strips 6½″ × WOF; subcut into 4 rectangles 6½″ × 12½″ (background), 4 rectangles 2½″ × 4½″ (D-12″), 32 rectangles 1½″ × 2½″ (D-6″).

F (6″, 12″): Cut 1 strip 4½″ × WOF; subcut into 1 square 4½″ × 4½″ (F-12″), 8 squares 2½″ × 2½″ (F-6″).

110 Blocks

3 Annie's Choice

 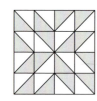 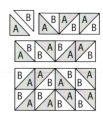 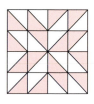

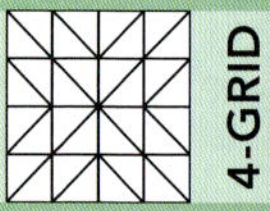

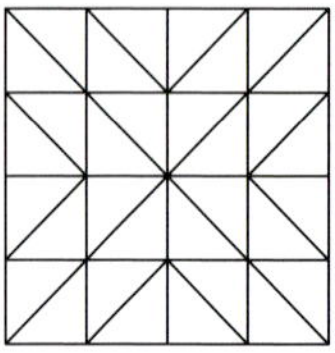

FOR	CUT	NEED	4"	6"	8"	10"	12"
A	8	16	1⅞	2⅜	2⅞	3⅜	3⅞
B	8	16	1⅞	2⅜	2⅞	3⅜	3⅞

DESIGN OPTIONS

PRECUT FRIENDLY!

Each 14" block uses:

FQ × ½ fat quarter for A

FQ × ½ fat quarter for B

YARDAGE FOR QUEEN QUILT

84" × 98"

14" block

6 × 7 setting = 42 blocks

A, B: 42 fat quarters

CUTTING

NOTE *Mix and match sets of A and B to make each block.*

From each fat quarter, cut 4 strips 4⅜" × WOFQ; subcut 8 squares 4⅜" × 4⅜" (A) and 8 squares 4⅜" × 4⅜" (B).

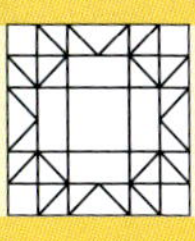

Arizona Star 4

6-GRID

   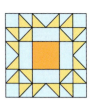

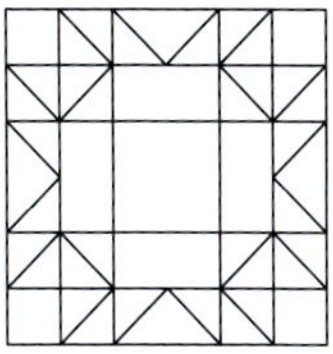

FOR	CUT	NEED	3″	6″	9″	12″	15″
A	4	4	1	1½	2	2½	3
B	10	20	1⅜	1⅞	2⅜	2⅞	3⅜
C	6	12	1⅜	1⅞	2⅜	2⅞	3⅜
D	1	4	2¼	3¼	4¼	5¼	6¼
E	4	4	1 × 1½	1½ × 2½	2 × 3½	2½ × 4½	3 × 5½
F	1	1	1½	2½	3½	4½	5½

DESIGN OPTIONS

PRECUT FRIENDLY!

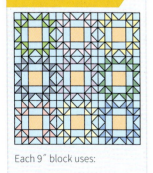

Each 9″ block uses:

| Jelly roll | × ⅔ strip for B

YARDAGE FOR LAP QUILT

54″ × 54″

9″ block

6 × 6 setting = 36 blocks

A, C, D, E: 2⅝ yards

B: 36 jelly roll strips

F: ½ yard

CUTTING

A: Cut 7 strips 2″ × WOF; subcut into 144 squares 2″ × 2″.

C: Cut 13 strips 2⅜″ × WOF; subcut into 216 squares 2⅜″ × 2⅜″.

D: Cut 4 strips 4¼″ × WOF; subcut into 36 squares 4¼″ × 4¼″.

E: Cut 12 strips 2″ × WOF; subcut into 144 rectangles 2″ × 3½″.

B: From each jelly roll strip, cut 10 squares 2⅜″ × 2⅜″.

F: Cut 3 strips 3½″ × WOF; subcut into 36 squares 3½″ × 3½″.

110 Blocks

5 Arkansas Star

3-GRID

 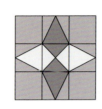 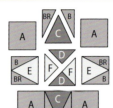 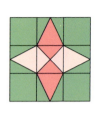

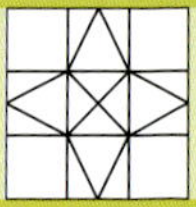

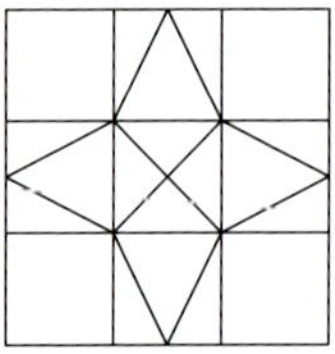

FOR	CUT	NEED	3″	6″	9″	12″	15″
A	4 ▭	4 ▭	1½	2½	3½	4½	5½
B*	2 ▭	4 ◩	1½ × 1¾	2¼ × 2½	2¾ × 3½	3¼ × 4½	3¾ × 5½
BR*	2 ▭	4 ◩	1½ × 1¾	2¼ × 2½	2¾ × 3½	3¼ × 4½	3¾ × 5½
C*	2 ▭	2 △	1½ × 1⅞	2½ × 2⅞	3½ × 3⅞	4½ × 4⅞	5½ × 5⅞
D	1 ▭	2 ⊠	2¼	3¼	4¼	5¼	6¼
E*	2 ▭	2 △	1½ × 1⅞	2½ × 2⅞	3½ × 3⅞	4½ × 4⅞	5½ × 5⅞
F	1 ▭	2 ⊠	2¼	3¼	4¼	5¼	6¼

* Refer to Triangle in a Square (page 122).

DESIGN OPTIONS

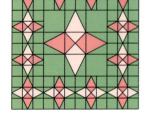

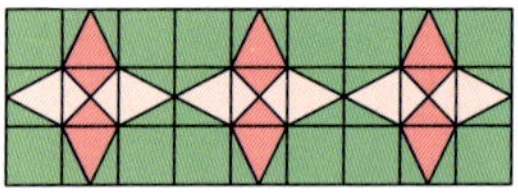

YARDAGE FOR TABLE TOPPER

24″ × 24″

6″ and 12″ blocks

13 blocks

A, B, BR: ¾ yard

C, D: ½ yard

E, F: ½ yard

CUTTING

A (12″), B & BR (12″): Cut 1 strip 4½″ × WOF; subcut into 4 squares 4½″ × 4½″ (A) and 4 rectangles 3¼″ × 4½″ (2B, 2BR).

A (6″), B & BR (6″): Cut 3 strips 2½″ × WOF; subcut 48 squares 2½″ × 2½″ (A). Cut 3 strips 2¼″ × WOF; subcut 48 rectangles 2¼″ × 2½″ (24B, 24BR).

C (12″), D (6″, 12″): Cut 1 strip 5¼″ × WOF; subcut into 1 square 5¼″ × 5¼″ (D-12″), 2 rectangles 4½″ × 4⅞″ (C), and 6 squares 3¼″ × 3¼″ (D-6″).

C, 6″: Cut 2 strips 2½″ × WOF; subcut 24 rectangles 2½″ × 2⅞″.

E (12″), F (6″, 12″): Cut 1 strip 5¼″ × WOF; subcut into 1 square 5¼″ × 5¼″ (F-12″), 2 rectangles 4½″ × 4⅞″ (E), and 6 squares 3¼″ × 3¼″ (F-6″).

E, 6″: Cut 2 strips 2½″ × WOF; subcut 24 rectangles 2½″ × 2⅞″.

8-GRID

Arrowheads 6

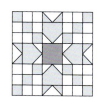
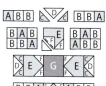
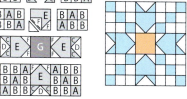

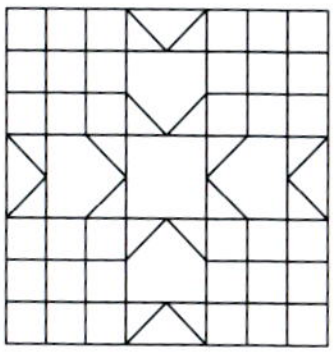

FOR	CUT	NEED	4″	6″	8″	10″	12″
A	12	12	1	1¼	1½	1¾	2
B	24	24	1	1¼	1½	1¾	2
C	4	8	1⅜	1⅝	1⅞	2⅛	2⅜
D	1	4	2¼	2¾	3¼	3¾	4¼
E	4	4	1½	2	2½	3	3½
F*	8	8	1	1¼	1½	1¾	2
G	1	1	1½	2	2½	3	3½

Refer to Sewing Squares to Squares or Rectangles (page 123)

DESIGN OPTIONS

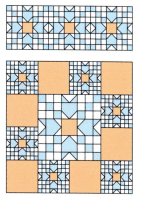

YARDAGE FOR WALL HANGING

24″ × 24″

6″ and 12″ blocks

6 × 6″ + 1 × 12″ = 7 blocks plus background blocks

A, C, E: ½ yard

B, D, F: ⅝ yard

G, background: ⅜ yard

CUTTING

A (6″, 12″): Cut 1 strip 2″ × WOF; subcut into 12 squares 2″ × 2″ (6″) and 14 squares 1¼″ × 1¼″ (12″).

A, 6″: Cut 2 strips 1¼″ × WOF; subcut 58 squares 1¼″ × 1¼″.

C, 12″: Cut 1 strip 2⅜″ × WOF; subcut into 4 squares 2⅜″ × 2⅜″.

C, 6″: Cut 1 strip 1⅝″ × WOF; subcut 24 squares 1⅝″ × 1⅝″.

E (6″, 12″): Cut 1 strip 3½″ × WOF; subcut into 4 squares 3½″ × 3½″ (6″) and 3 squares 2″ × 2″ (12″).

E, 6″: Cut 1 strip 2″ × WOF; subcut into 21 squares 2″ × 2″.

B (6″, 12″): Cut 2 strips 2″ × WOF; subcut into 24 squares 2″ × 2″ (12″) and 12 squares 1¼″ × 1¼″ (6″).

B, 6″: Cut 4 strips 1¼″ × WOF; subcut 132 squares 1¼″ × 1¼″.

D (6″, 12″): Cut 1 strip 4¼″ × WOF; subcut 1 square 4¼″ × 4¼″ (12″) and 6 squares 2¾″ × 2¾″ (6″).

F, 6″: Cut 2 strips 1¼″ × WOF; subcut 48 squares 1¼″ × 1¼″.

F, 12″: Cut 1 strip 2″ × WOF; subcut into 8 squares 2″ × 2″.

G (6″, 12″): Cut 1 strip 3½″ × WOF; subcut into 1 square 3½″ × 3½″ (12″) and 6 squares 2″ × 2″ (6″).

Background: Cut 1 strip 6½″ × WOF; subcut 6 squares 6½″ × 6½″.

7 Aunt Eliza's Star

3-GRID

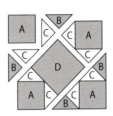
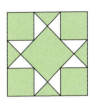

FOR	CUT	NEED	3″	6″	9″	12″	15″
A	4	4	1½	2½	3½	4½	5½
B	1	4 ⊠	2¼	3¼	4¼	5¼	6¼
C	2	8 ⊠	2¼	3¼	4¼	5¼	6¼
D	1	1	1⅞	3⅜	4¾	6¼	7½

DESIGN OPTIONS

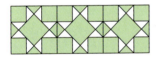

PRECUT FRIENDLY!

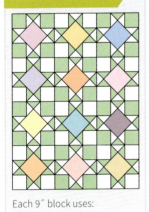

Each 9″ block uses:

CS × 1 square for D

YARDAGE FOR TWIN QUILT

63″ × 90″

9″ block

7 × 10 setting = 70 blocks

D: 70 charm squares

Fabric 1: 2¾ yards

Fabric 2: 2¾ yards

CUTTING

D: Trim each charm square to 4¾″ × 4¾″.

From each fabric:

A: Cut 12 strips 3½″ × WOF; subcut into 140 squares 3½″ × 3½″.

B: Cut 4 strips 4¼″ × WOF; subcut into 35 squares 4¼″ × 4¼″.

C: Cut 8 strips 4¼″ × WOF; subcut into 70 squares 4¼″ × 4¼″.

Best Of All 8

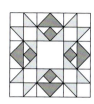

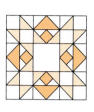

FOR	CUT	NEED	3″	6″	9″	12″	15″
A	8	8	1	1½	2	2½	3
B	8	16	1⅜	1⅞	2⅜	2⅞	3⅜
C	8	16	1⅜	1⅞	2⅜	2⅞	3⅜
D	1	4	2¼	3¼	4¼	5¼	6¼
E	2	8	1¾	2¼	2¾	3¼	3¾
F	4	4	⅞	1¼	1½	1⅞	2¼
G	1	1	1½	2½	3½	4½	5½

DESIGN OPTIONS

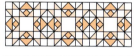
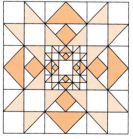

YARDAGE FOR TABLE TOPPER

27″ × 27″

9″ and 27″ blocks

2 blocks

A, C, E, G: ¾ yard

B: ½ yard

D, F: ⅜ yard

CUTTING

A, 27″: Cut 1 strip 5″ × WOF; subcut into 8 squares 5″ × 5″.

C, 27″: Cut 1 strip 5⅜″ × WOF; subcut into 7 squares 5⅜″ × 5⅜″.

A (9″), C (9″): Cut 1 strip 2⅜″ × WOF; subcut into 8 squares 2⅜″ × 2⅜″ (C) and 8 squares 2″ × 2″ (A).

C (27″), E (9″, 27″), G (9″): Cut 1 strip 5¾″ × WOF; subcut into 2 squares 5¾″ × 5¾″ (E-27″), 1 square 5⅜″ × 5⅜″ (C), 2 squares 2¾″ × 2¾″ (E-9″), and 1 square 3½″ × 3½″ (G).

B (9″, 27″): Cut 2 strips 5⅜″ × WOF; subcut 8 squares 5⅜″ × 5⅜″ (27″) and 8 squares 2⅜″ × 2⅜″ (9″).

D (9″, 27″), F (9″, 27″): Cut 1 strip 10¼″ × WOF; subcut 1 square 10¼″ × 10¼″ (D-27″), 1 square 4¼″ × 4¼″ (D-9″), 4 squares 3¾″ × 3¾″ (F-27″), and 4 squares 1½″ × 1½″ (F-9″).

9 Bethlehem Star

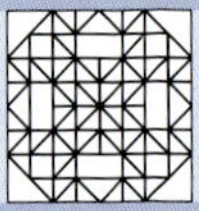

8-GRID

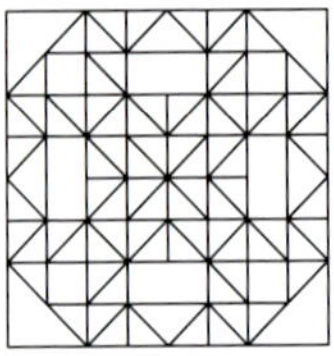

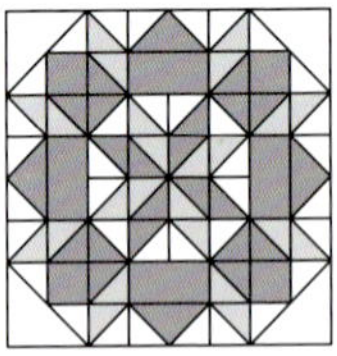

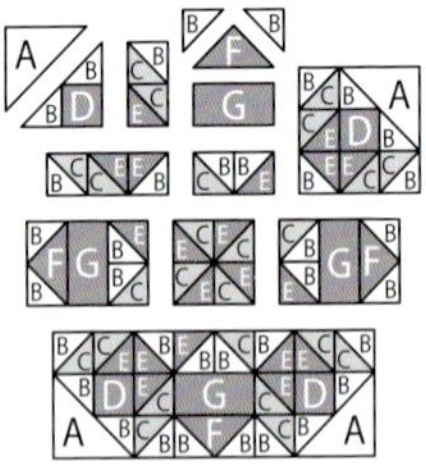

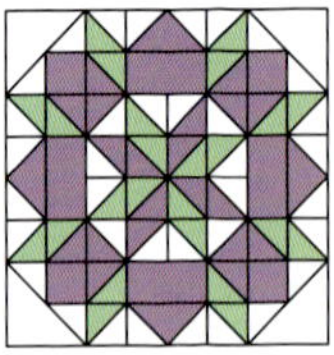

FOR	CUT	NEED	4″	6″	8″	10″	12″
A	2	4	1⅞	2⅜	2⅞	3⅜	3⅞
B	18	36	1⅜	1⅝	1⅞	2⅛	2⅜
C	12	24	1⅜	1⅝	1⅞	2⅛	2⅜
D	4	4	1	1¼	1½	1¾	2
E	10	20	1⅜	1⅝	1⅞	2⅛	2⅜
F	1	4	2¼	2¾	3¼	3¾	4¼
G	4	4	1 × 1½	1¼ × 2	1½ × 2½	1¾ × 3	2 × 3½

DESIGN OPTIONS

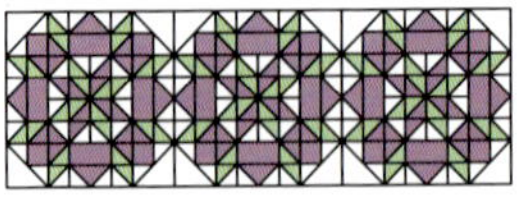

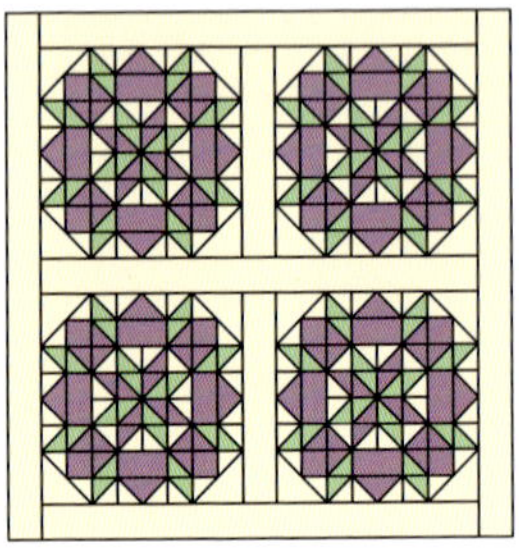

YARDAGE FOR WALL HANGING

30″ × 30″

12″ block

2 × 2 setting = 4 blocks

A, B, sashing, border: 1 yard

C: ⅓ yard

D, E, F, G: ½ yard

CUTTING

A: Cut 1 strip 3⅞″ × WOF; subcut into 8 squares 3⅞″ × 3⅞″.

B: Cut 5 strips 2⅜″ × WOF; subcut into 72 squares 2⅜″ × 2⅜″.

Sashing, border: Cut 5 strips 2½″ × WOF; subcut 2 rectangles 2½″ × 30½″, 3 rectangles 2½″ × 26½″, and 2 rectangles 2½″ × 12½″.

C: Cut 3 strips 2⅜″ × WOF; subcut into 48 squares 2⅜″ × 2⅜″.

D: Cut 1 strip 2″ × WOF; subcut into 16 squares 2″ × 2″.

E: Cut 2 strips 2⅜″ × WOF; subcut into 34 squares 2⅜″ × 2⅜″.

E, F: Cut 1 strip 4¼″ × WOF; subcut into 4 squares 4¼″ × 4¼″ (F) and 6 squares 2⅜″ × 2⅜″ (E).

G: Cut 1 strip 3½″ × WOF; subcut into 16 rectangles 2″ × 3½″.

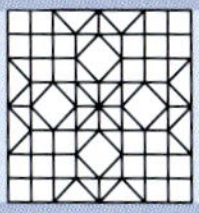

Black Diamond 10

8-GRID

 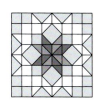 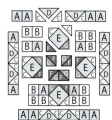 

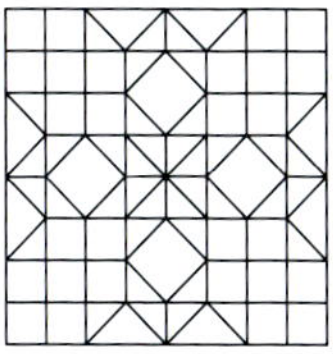

FOR	CUT	NEED	4″	6″	8″	10″	12″
A	16	16	1	1¼	1½	1¾	2
B	12	12	1	1¼	1½	1¾	2
C	12	24	1⅜	1⅝	1⅞	2⅛	2⅜
D	2	8	2¼	2¾	3¼	3¾	4¼
E	4	4	1¼	1½	1⅞	2¼	2⅝
F	4	8	1⅜	1⅝	1⅞	2⅛	2⅜
G	4	8	1⅜	1⅝	1⅞	2⅛	2⅜

DESIGN OPTIONS

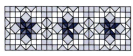

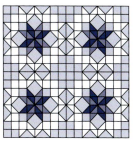

YARDAGE FOR WALL HANGING

24″ × 24″

12″ block

2 × 2 setting = 4 blocks

A, D, E: ½ yard

B, C: ½ yard

F: ⅛ yard

G: ⅛ yard

CUTTING

A: Cut 3 strips 2″ × WOF; subcut into 63 squares 2″ × 2″.

A, D: Cut 1 strip 4¼″ × WOF; subcut 8 squares 4¼″ × 4¼″ (D) and 1 square 2″ × 2″ (A).

E: Cut 1 strip 2⅝″ × WOF; subcut into 16 squares 2⅝″ × 2⅝″.

B: Cut 3 strips 2″ × WOF; subcut into 48 squares 2″ × 2″.

C: Cut 3 strips 2⅜″ × WOF; subcut into 48 squares 2⅜″ × 2⅜″.

F: Cut 1 strip 2⅜″ × WOF; subcut into 16 squares 2⅜″ × 2⅜″.

G: Cut 1 strip 2⅜″ × WOF; subcut into 16 squares 2⅜″ × 2⅜″.

11 Boxes and Baskets

6-GRID

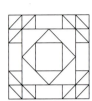
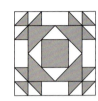
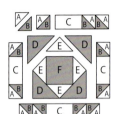

FOR	CUT	NEED	3"	6"	9"	12"	15"
A	6	12	1 3/8	1 7/8	2 3/8	2 7/8	3 3/8
B	6	12	1 3/8	1 7/8	2 3/8	2 7/8	3 3/8
C	4	4	1 × 1 1/2	1 1/2 × 2 1/2	2 × 3 1/2	2 1/2 × 4 1/2	3 × 5 1/2
D	2	4	1 7/8	2 7/8	3 7/8	4 7/8	5 7/8
E	1	4	2 1/4	3 1/4	4 1/4	5 1/4	6 1/4
F	1	1	1 1/2	2 1/2	3 1/2	4 1/2	5 1/2

DESIGN OPTIONS

PRECUT FRIENDLY!

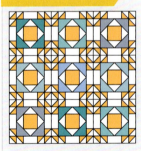

Each 12" block uses:

LC × 1/2 square for D

YARDAGE FOR DOUBLE QUILT

84" × 84"

12" block

7 × 7 setting = 49 blocks

A, C, E: 4 1/2 yards

B, F: 2 5/8 yards

D: 25 layer cake squares

CUTTING

A: Cut 21 strips 2 7/8" × WOF; subcut into 294 squares 2 7/8" × 2 7/8".

C: Cut 22 strips 2 1/2" × WOF; subcut into 196 rectangles 2 1/2" × 4 1/2.

E: Cut 7 strips 5 1/4" × WOF; subcut into 49 squares 5 1/4" × 5 1/4".

B: Cut 21 strips 2 7/8" × WOF; subcut into 294 squares 2 7/8" × 2 7/8".

F: Cut 6 strips 4 1/2" × WOF; subcut into 49 squares 4 1/2" × 4 1/2.

D: Cut each layer cake square into 4 squares 4 7/8" × 4 7/8".

Quick & Easy All Stars Block Tool

Bright Stars 12

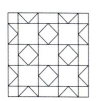 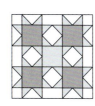 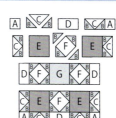 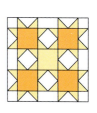

FOR	CUT	NEED	4"	6"	8"	10"	12"
A	4	4	1	1¼	1½	1¾	2
B	16	32	1⅜	1⅝	1⅞	2⅛	2⅜
C	2	8	2¼	2¾	3¼	3¾	4¼
D	4	4	1 × 1½	1¼ × 2	1½ × 2½	1¾ × 3	2 × 3½
E	4	4	1½	2	2½	3	3½
F	4	4	1¼	1½	1⅞	2¼	2⅝
G	1	1	1½	2	2½	3	3½

DESIGN OPTIONS

YARDAGE FOR LAP QUILT

66" × 66"

12" block

5 × 5 setting = 25 blocks with sashing and cornerstones

A, C, D, F: 2⅛ yards

B, G, cornerstones: 2 yards

E, sashing: 1¾ yards

CUTTING

A: Cut 5 strips 2" × WOF; subcut into 100 squares 2" × 2".

C: Cut 6 strips 4¼" × WOF; subcut into 50 squares 4¼" × 4¼".

D: Cut 5 strips 3½" × WOF; subcut into 100 rectangles 2" × 3½".

F: Cut 7 strips 2⅝" × WOF; subcut into 100 squares 2⅝" × 2⅝".

B: Cut 24 strips 2⅜" × WOF; subcut into 400 squares 2⅜" × 2⅜".

G, cornerstones: Cut 3 strips 3½" × WOF; subcut into 25 squares 3½" × 3½" (G) and 16 squares 2" × 2" (cornerstones).

E: Cut 9 strips 3½" × WOF; subcut into 100 squares 3½" × 3½".

Sashing: Cut 2 strips 12½" × WOF; subcut into 40 rectangles 2" × 12½".

13 Broken Star

4-GRID

 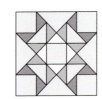 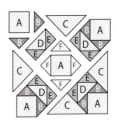 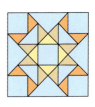

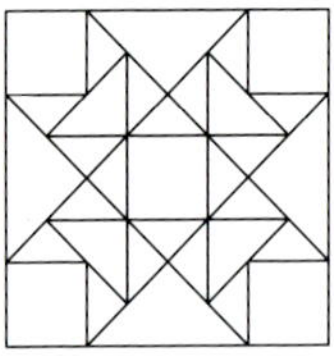

FOR	CUT	NEED	4"	6"	8"	10"	12"
A	5	5	1½	2	2½	3	3½
B	2	8	2¼	2¾	3¼	3¾	4¼
C	1	4	3¼	4¼	5¼	6¼	7¼
D	2	4	1⅞	2⅜	2⅞	3⅜	3⅞
E	2	8	2¼	2¾	3¼	3¾	4¼
F	1	4	2¼	2¾	3¼	3¾	4¼

DESIGN OPTIONS

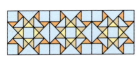
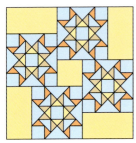

YARDAGE FOR WALL HANGING

30" × 30"

12" block

4 pieced blocks plus background blocks

A, C, D: ⅝ yard

B: ¼ yard

E: ¼ yard

F, background: ½ yard

CUTTING

A: Cut 2 strips 3½" × WOF; subcut into 20 squares 3½" × 3½".

C: Cut 1 strip 7¼" × WOF; subcut into 4 squares 7¼" × 7¼".

D: Cut 1 strip 3⅞" × WOF; subcut into 8 squares 3⅞" × 3⅞".

B: Cut 1 strip 4¼" × WOF; subcut into 8 squares 4¼" × 4¼".

E: Cut 1 strip 4¼" × WOF; subcut into 8 squares 4¼" × 4¼".

F, background: Cut 2 strips 6½" × WOF; subcut into 4 rectangles 6½" × 12½", 1 square 6½" × 6½" (background), and 4 squares 4¼" × 4¼" (F).

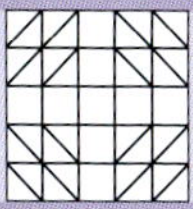

Christmas Star 14

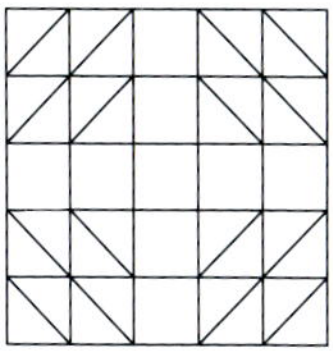

5-GRID

 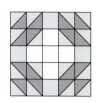 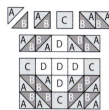 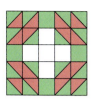

FOR	CUT	NEED	5″	7½″	10″	12½″	15″
A	8	16	1⅞	2⅜	2⅞	3⅜	3⅞
B	8	16	1⅞	2⅜	2⅞	3⅜	3⅞
C	4	4	1½	2	2½	3	3½
D	5	5	1½	2	2½	3	3½

DESIGN OPTIONS

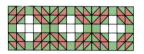

PRECUT FRIENDLY!

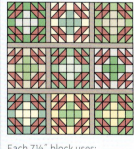

Each 7½″ block uses:

Jelly roll × ½ strip for A

Jelly roll × ¼ strip for C

Jelly roll × ¼ strip for D

YARDAGE FOR TWIN QUILT

67″ × 84″

7½″ block

8 × 10 setting = 80 blocks

A, C, D: 80 jelly roll strips

B: 2¾ yards

Sashing: 1⅜ yards

CUTTING

A, C, D: From each jelly roll strip, subcut 8 squares 2⅜″ × 2⅜″ (A), 4 squares 2″ × 2″ (C) and 5 squares 2″ × 2″ (D).

B: Cut 38 strips 2⅜″ × WOF; subcut into 640 squares 2⅜″ × 2⅜″.

Sashing: Cut 14 strips 1½″ × WOF; subcut into 70 rectangles 1½″ × 8″. Cut 15 strips 1½″ × WOF; sew together and subcut into 9 rectangles 1½″ × 67½″.

110 Blocks   25

15 Combination Star

   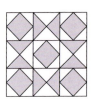

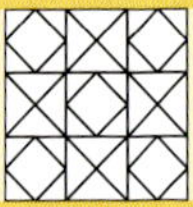

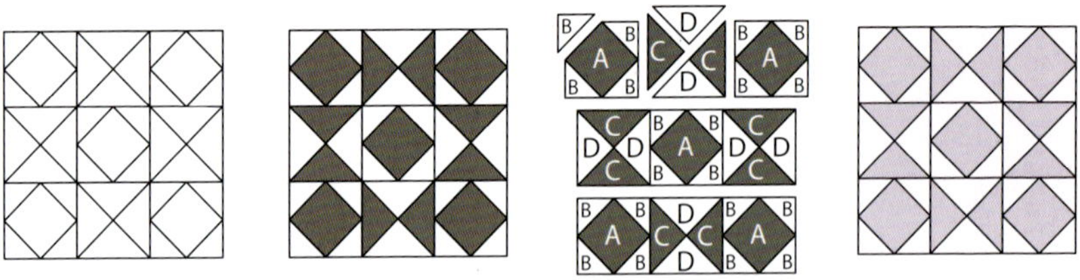

FOR	CUT	NEED	3″	6″	9″	12″	15″
A	5 ■	5 ■	1¼	1⅞	2⅝	3⅜	4
B	10 □	20 ◨	1⅜	1⅞	2⅜	2⅞	3⅜
C	2 ■	8 ⊠	2¼	3¼	4¼	5¼	6¼
D	2 □	8 ⊠	2¼	3¼	4¼	5¼	6¼

DESIGN OPTIONS

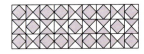

PRECUT FRIENDLY!

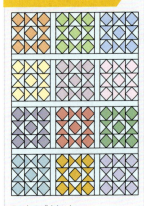

Each 21″ block uses:

FQ × 1 fat quarter for A, C

YARDAGE FOR TWIN QUILT

69″ × 93″

21″ block

3 × 4 setting = 12 blocks plus sashing

A, C: 12 fat quarters

B, D, sashing: 4¼ yards

CUTTING

A, C: From each fat quarter, cut: 2 squares 8¼″ × 8¼″ (C) and 5 squares 5½″ × 5½″ (A).

B: Cut 14 strips 4⅜″ × WOF; subcut into 120 squares 4⅜″ × 4⅜″.

D: Cut 5 strips 8¼″ × WOF; subcut into 24 squares 8¼″ × 8¼″.

Sashing: Cut 8 strips 3½″ × WOF; subcut into 8 rectangles 3½″ × 21½″. (Set aside 6 leftover 3½″ × 20½″ strips.) Cut 3 strips 3½″ × WOF; sew 2 leftover 3½″ × 20½″ strips from above to each of these 3 WOF strips, then trim each to 69½″.

Constellation 16

4-GRID

  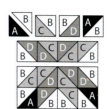 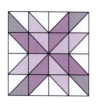

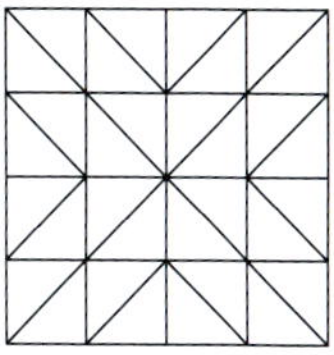

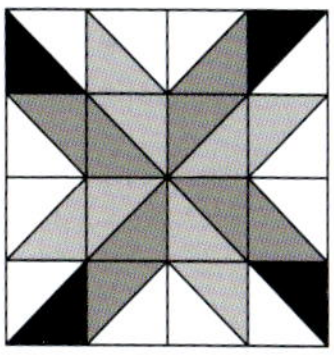

FOR	CUT	NEED	4"	6"	8"	10"	12"
A	2	4	1⅞	2⅜	2⅞	3⅜	3⅞
B	6	12	1⅞	2⅜	2⅞	3⅜	3⅞
C	4	8	1⅞	2⅜	2⅞	3⅜	3⅞
D	4	8	1⅞	2⅜	2⅞	3⅜	3⅞

DESIGN OPTIONS

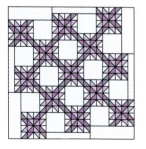

YARDAGE FOR LAP QUILT

60″ × 60″

12″ block

3 × 3 offset setting = 13 blocks plus alternate and background blocks

A: ½ yard

B, alternate blocks, borders: 2⅝ yards

C: ¾ yard

D: ¾ yard

CUTTING

A: Cut 3 strips 3⅞″ × WOF; subcut into 26 squares 3⅞″ × 3⅞″.

B: Cut 8 strips 3⅞″ × WOF; subcut into 78 squares 3⅞″ × 3⅞″.

Alternate blocks: Cut 3 strips 9½″ × WOF; subcut into 12 squares 9½″ × 9½″.

Borders: Cut 1 strip 21½″ × WOF; subcut into 4 rectangles 6½″ × 21½″ and 4 rectangles 3½″ × 21½″.

C: Cut 6 strips 3⅞″ × WOF; subcut into 52 squares 3⅞″ × 3⅞″.

D: Cut 6 strips 3⅞″ × WOF; subcut into 52 squares 3⅞″ × 3⅞″.

17 Contrary Wife

 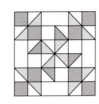 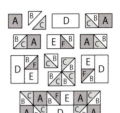

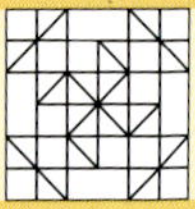

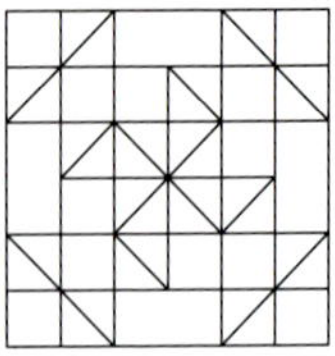

FOR	CUT	NEED	3″	6″	9″	12″	15″
A	8	8	1	1½	2	2½	3
B	8	16	1³⁄₈	1⅞	2³⁄₈	2⅞	3³⁄₈
C	6	12	1³⁄₈	1⅞	2³⁄₈	2⅞	3³⁄₈
D	4	4	1 × 1½	1½ × 2½	2 × 3½	2½ × 4½	3 × 5½
E	4	4	1	1½	2	2½	3
F	2	4	1³⁄₈	1⅞	2³⁄₈	2⅞	3³⁄₈

DESIGN OPTIONS

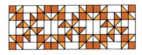

PRECUT FRIENDLY!

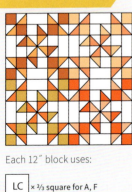

Each 12″ block uses:

LC × ⅔ square for A, F

LC × ⅓ square for C

YARDAGE FOR TWIN QUILT

72″ × 84″

12″ block

6 × 7 setting = 42 blocks

A, F: 42 layer cake squares

B, D, E: 4¼ yards

C: 42 layer cake squares

CUTTING

NOTE *Mix and match sets of 8A and 2F with 6C for each block.*

A, F: From each of 42 layer cake squares, cut 8 squares 2½″ × 2½″ (A) and 2 squares 2⅞″ × 2⅞″ (F).

B: Cut 24 strips 2⅞″ × WOF; subcut into 336 squares 2⅞″ × 2⅞″.

D: Cut 19 strips 2½″ × WOF; subcut into 168 rectangles 2½″ × 4½″.

E: Cut 11 strips 2½″ × WOF; subcut into 168 squares 2½″ × 2½″.

C: From each of 42 layer cake squares, cut 6 squares 2⅞″ × 2⅞″.

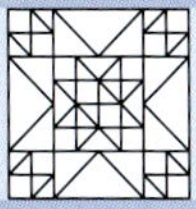

8-GRID

Coronation Star   18

 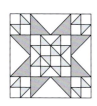 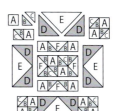 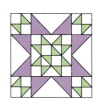

FOR	CUT	NEED	4″	6″	8″	10″	12″
A	14 ☐	14 ☐	1	1¼	1½	1¾	2
B	9 ☐	18 ◩	1⅜	1⅝	1⅞	2⅛	2⅜
C	5 ☐	10 ◩	1⅜	1⅝	1⅞	2⅛	2⅜
D	4 ☐	8 ◩	1⅞	2⅜	2⅞	3⅜	3⅞
E	1 ☐	4 ⊠	3¼	4¼	5¼	6¼	7¼
F	1 ☐	4 ⊠	2¼	2¾	3¼	3¾	4¼

DESIGN OPTIONS

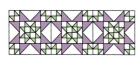

YARDAGE FOR BABY QUILT

36″ × 36″

12″ block

3 × 3 setting = 9 blocks

A, C, E, F: 1¼ yards

B: ½ yard

D: ⅝ yard

CUTTING

A: Cut 6 strips 2″ × WOF; subcut into 126 squares 2″ × 2″.

C: Cut 3 strips 2⅜″ × WOF; subcut into 45 squares 2⅜″ × 2⅜″.

E: Cut 2 strips 7¼″ × WOF; subcut into 9 squares 7¼″ × 7¼″.

F: Cut 1 strip 4¼″ × WOF; subcut into 9 squares 4¼″ × 4¼″.

B: Cut 5 strips 2⅜″ × WOF; subcut into 81 squares 2⅜″ × 2⅜″.

D: Cut 4 strips 3⅞″ × WOF; subcut into 36 squares 3⅞″ × 3⅞″.

110 Blocks

19 Country Star

3-GRID

 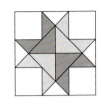  

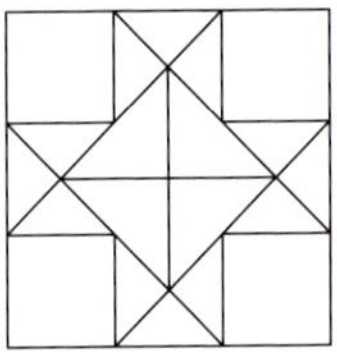

FOR	CUT	NEED	3″	6″	9″	12″	15″
A	4 □	4 □	1½	2½	3½	4½	5½
B	1 ■	4 ⊠	2¼	3¼	4¼	5¼	6¼
C	1 □	4 ⊠	2¼	3¼	4¼	5¼	6¼
D	1 □	4 ⊠	2¼	3¼	4¼	5¼	6¼
E	1 ■	2 ◩	1⅞	2⅞	3⅞	4⅞	5⅞
F	1 □	2 ◩	1⅞	2⅞	3⅞	4⅞	5⅞

DESIGN OPTIONS

PRECUT FRIENDLY!

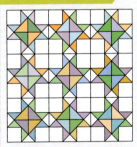

Each 9″ block uses:

CS	× 1 square for B
CS	× 1 square for D
CS	× 1 square for E
CS	× 1 square for F

YARDAGE FOR BABY QUILT

36″ × 36″

9″ block

4 × 4 setting = 16 blocks

A, C: 1 yard

B, D, E, F: 64 charm squares

CUTTING

A: Cut 6 strips 3½″ × WOF; subcut into 64 squares 3½″ × 3½″.

C: Cut 2 strips 4¼″ × WOF; subcut into 16 squares 4¼″ × 4¼″.

B, D: Trim 32 charm squares to 4¼″ × 4¼″.

E, F: Trim 32 charm squares to 3⅞″ × 3⅞″.

8-GRID

Cozy Star 20

  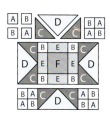 

FOR	CUT	NEED	4″	6″	8″	10″	12″
A	8 ☐	8 ☐	1	1¼	1½	1¾	2
B	12 ☐	12 ☐	1	1¼	1½	1¾	2
C	4 ☐	8 ◺	1⅞	2⅜	2⅞	3⅜	3⅞
D	1 ☐	4 ⊠	3¼	4¼	5¼	6¼	7¼
E	4 ▭	4 ▭	1 × 1½	1¼ × 2	1½ × 2½	1¾ × 3	2 × 3½
F	1 ☐	1 ☐	1½	2	2½	3	3½

DESIGN OPTIONS

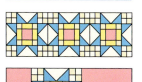

YARDAGE FOR BABY QUILT

30″ × 30″

12″ block

4 blocks plus background blocks

A, D: ⅜ yard

B: ¼ yard

C: ⅓ yard

E: ¼ yard

F, background: ½ yard

CUTTING

A: Cut 2 strips 2″ × WOF; subcut into 32 squares 2″ × 2″.

D: Cut 1 strip 7¼″ × WOF; subcut into 4 squares 7¼″ × 7¼″.

B: Cut 3 strips 2″ × WOF; subcut into 48 squares 2″ × 2″.

C: Cut 2 strips 3⅞″ × WOF; subcut into 16 squares 3⅞″ × 3⅞″.

E: Cut 1 strip 3½″ × WOF; subcut into 16 rectangles 2″ × 3½″.

F, background: Cut 1 strip 12½″ × WOF; subcut into 4 rectangles 6½″ × 12½″ (background), 1 square 6½″ × 6½″ (background), and 4 squares 3½″ × 3½″ (F).

21 Cross and Star

8-GRID

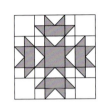
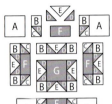
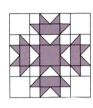

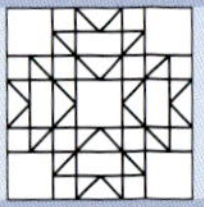

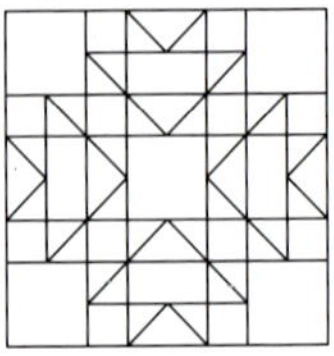

FOR	CUT	NEED	4″	6″	8″	10″	12″
A	4 □	4 □	1½	2	2½	3	3½
B	12 □	12 □	1	1¼	1½	1¾	2
C	4 □	8 ◨	1⅜	1⅝	1⅞	2⅛	2⅜
D	12 ▦	24 ◨	1⅜	1⅝	1⅞	2⅛	2⅜
E	2 □	8 ⊠	2¼	2¾	3¼	3¾	4¼
F	4 ▭	4 ▭	1 × 1½	1¼ × 2	1½ × 2½	1¾ × 3	2 × 3½
G	1 ▦	1 ▦	1½	2	2½	3	3½

DESIGN OPTIONS

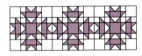

PRECUT FRIENDLY!

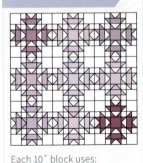

Each 10″ block uses:

LC × 1 square for D, F, G

YARDAGE FOR LAP QUILT

60″ × 60″

10″ block

6 × 6 setting = 36 blocks

A, B, C, E: 3⅛ yards

D, F, G: 36 layer cake squares

CUTTING

A: Cut 11 strips 3″ × WOF; subcut into 144 squares 3″ × 3″.

B: Cut 18 strips 1¾″ × WOF; subcut into 432 squares 1¾″ × 1¾″.

C: Cut 8 strips 2⅛″ × WOF; subcut into 144 squares 2⅛″ × 2⅛″.

E: Cut 7 strips 3¾″ × WOF; subcut into 72 squares 3¾″ × 3¾″.

D, F, G: From each layer cake square, cut 12 squares 2⅛″ × 2⅛″ (D), 4 rectangles 1¾″ × 3″ (F), and 1 square 3″ × 3″ (G).

6-GRID

Crystal Star 22

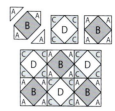
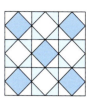

FOR	CUT	NEED	3"	6"	9"	12"	15"
A	10	20	1 3/8	1 7/8	2 3/8	2 7/8	3 3/8
B	5	5	1 1/4	1 7/8	2 5/8	3 3/8	4
C	8	16	1 3/8	1 7/8	2 3/8	2 7/8	3 3/8
D	4	4	1 1/4	1 7/8	2 5/8	3 3/8	4

DESIGN OPTIONS

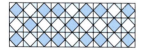
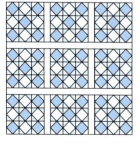

YARDAGE FOR LAP QUILT

68" × 68"

12" block

5 × 5 setting = 25 blocks

A, D, sashing: 3 3/8 yards

B: 1 1/4 yards

C: 1 3/8 yard

CUTTING

A: Cut 18 strips 2 7/8" × WOF; subcut into 250 squares 2 7/8" × 2 7/8".

D: Cut 9 strips 3 3/8" × WOF; subcut into 100 squares 3 3/8" × 3 3/8".

Sashing: Cut 14 strips 2 1/2" × WOF; subcut 7 into 20 rectangles 2 1/2" × 12 1/2", sew 7 together and subcut into 4 strips 2 1/2" × 68 1/2".

B: Cut 11 strips 3 3/8" × WOF; subcut into 125 squares 3 3/8" × 3 3/8".

C: Cut 15 strips 2 7/8" × WOF; subcut into 200 squares 2 7/8" × 2 7/8".

23 Diamond Ripple

FOR	CUT	NEED	3"	6"	9"	12"	15"
A	12	24	1³⁄₈	1⁷⁄₈	2³⁄₈	2⁷⁄₈	3³⁄₈
B	8	16	1³⁄₈	1⁷⁄₈	2³⁄₈	2⁷⁄₈	3³⁄₈
C	4	4	1¼	1⁷⁄₈	2⁵⁄₈	3³⁄₈	4
D	4	8	1³⁄₈	1⁷⁄₈	2³⁄₈	2⁷⁄₈	3³⁄₈
E	4	8	1³⁄₈	1⁷⁄₈	2³⁄₈	2⁷⁄₈	3³⁄₈

DESIGN OPTIONS

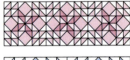
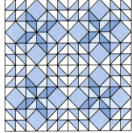

YARDAGE FOR BABY QUILT

30″ × 30″

15″ block

2 × 2 setting = 4 blocks

A: ½ yard

B, C: ⅝ yard

D: ⅓ yard

E: ⅓ yard

CUTTING

A: Cut 4 strips 3³⁄₈″ × WOF; subcut into 48 squares 3³⁄₈″ × 3³⁄₈″.

B: Cut 3 strips 3³⁄₈″ × WOF; subcut into 32 squares 3³⁄₈″ × 3³⁄₈″.

C: Cut 2 strips 4″ × WOF; subcut into 16 squares 4″ × 4″.

D: Cut 2 strips 3³⁄₈″ × WOF; subcut into 16 squares 3³⁄₈″ × 3³⁄₈″.

E: Cut 2 strips 3³⁄₈″ × WOF; subcut into 16 squares 3³⁄₈″ × 3³⁄₈″.

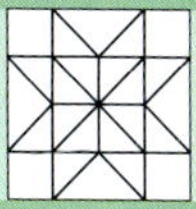

Diamond Star 24

4-GRID

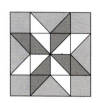
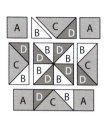

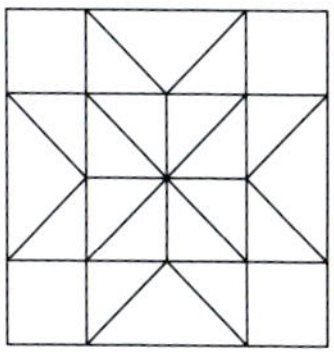

FOR	CUT	NEED	4″	6″	8″	10″	12″
A	4	4	1½	2	2½	3	3½
B	4	8	1⅞	2⅜	2⅞	3⅜	3⅞
C	1	4	3¼	4¼	5¼	6¼	7¼
D	4	8	1⅞	2⅜	2⅞	3⅜	3⅞

DESIGN OPTIONS

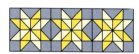
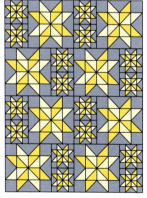

YARDAGE FOR BABY QUILT

36″ × 48″

12″ and 6″ blocks

16 × 6″ + 8 × 12″ = 24 blocks

A, C: 1¼ yards

B: ⅞ yard

D: ⅞ yard

CUTTING

A (6″, 12″): Cut 3 strips 3½″ × WOF; subcut into 32 squares 3½″ × 3½″ (12″) and 1 square 2″ × 2″ (6″).

A, 6″: Cut 3 strips 2″ × WOF; subcut into 63 squares 2″ × 2″.

C, 12″: Cut 2 strips 7¼″ × WOF; subcut into 8 squares 7¼″ × 7¼″.

C, 6″: Cut 2 strips 4¼″ × WOF; subcut into 16 squares 4¼″ × 4¼″.

B, 12″: Cut 4 strips 3⅞″ × WOF; subcut into 32 squares 3⅞″ × 3⅞″.

B, 6″: Cut 4 strips 2⅜″ × WOF; subcut into 64 squares 2⅜″ × 2⅜″.

D, 12″: Cut 4 strips 3⅞″ × WOF; subcut into 32 squares 3⅞″ × 3⅞″.

D, 6″: Cut 4 strips 2⅜″ × WOF; subcut into 64 squares 2⅜″ × 2⅜″.

25 Dolley Madison's Star

 3-GRID

 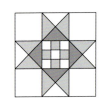 

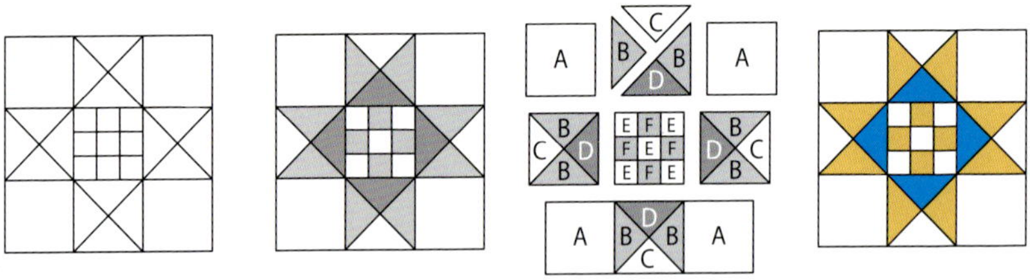

FOR	CUT	NEED	4½″	9″	13½″	18″	22½″
A	4 ☐	4 ☐	2	3½	5	6½	8
B	2 ☐	8 ⊠	2¾	4¼	5¾	7¼	8¾
C	1 ☐	4 ⊠	2¾	4¼	5¾	7¼	8¾
D	1 ☐	4 ⊠	2¾	4¼	5¾	7¼	8¾
E	5 ☐	5 ☐	1	1½	2	2½	3
F	4 ☐	4 ☐	1	1½	2	2½	3

DESIGN OPTIONS

PRECUT FRIENDLY!

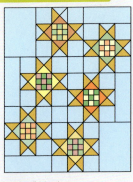

Each 9″ block uses:

CS × 1 square for D

CS × 1 square for E, F

YARDAGE FOR WALL HANGING

24″ × 30″

9″ block

6 blocks plus background

A, C, background: ¾ yard

B: ⅜ yard

D, E, F: 12 charm squares

CUTTING

NOTE *Mix and match sets of 5E and 4F for each block. Refer to Sewing Partial Seams (page 123).*

A: Cut 2 strips 3½″ × WOF; subcut into 24 squares 3½″ × 3½″.

C: Cut 1 strip 4¼″ × WOF; subcut into 6 squares 4¼″ × 4¼″.

Background: Cut 1 strip 7″ × WOF; subcut into 2 rectangles 6½″ × 9½″, 4 rectangles 3½″ × 9½″, and 2 squares 3½″ × 3½″.

B: Cut 2 strips 4¼″ × WOF; subcut into 12 squares 4¼″ × 4¼″.

D: Trim 6 charm squares to 4¼″ × 4¼″.

E, F: Trim each of 6 charm squares to 9 squares 1½″ × 1½″ (5E, 4F).

Quick & Easy All Stars Block Tool

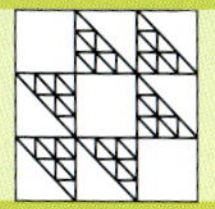

Double Pyramid — 26

3-GRID

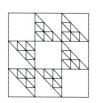 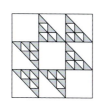 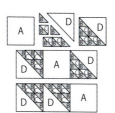 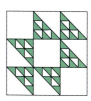

FOR	CUT	NEED	4½″	9″	13½″	18″	22½″
A	3	3	2	3½	5	6½	8
B	18	36	1⅜	1⅞	2⅜	2⅞	3⅜
C	9	18	1⅜	1⅞	2⅜	2⅞	3⅜
D	3	6	2⅜	3⅞	5⅜	6⅞	8⅜

DESIGN OPTIONS

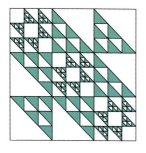

YARDAGE FOR WALL HANGING

27″ × 27″

9″ and 27″ blocks

3 × 9″ + 1 × 27″ = 4 blocks

A, C, D: 1 yard

B: ½ yard

CUTTING

A, 9″: Cut 1 strip 3½″ × WOF; subcut into 9 squares 3½″ × 3½″.

C, 27″: Cut 1 strip 3⅞″ × WOF; subcut into 9 squares 3⅞″ × 3⅞″.

C, 9″: Cut 2 strips 1⅞″ × WOF; subcut into 27 squares 1⅞″ × 1⅞″.

D, 27″: Cut 1 strip 9⅞″ × WOF; subcut into 3 squares 9⅞″ × 9⅞″.

D, 9″: Cut 1 strip 3⅞″ × WOF; subcut into 9 squares 3⅞″ × 3⅞″.

B, 27″: Cut 2 strips 3⅞″ × WOF; subcut into 18 squares 3⅞″ × 3⅞″.

B, 9″: Cut 3 strips 1⅞″ × WOF; subcut into 54 squares 1⅞″ × 1⅞″.

27 Double Sawtooth Star

  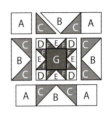 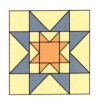

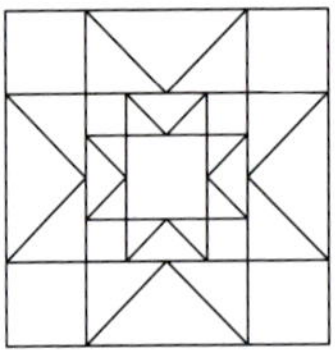

FOR	CUT	NEED	4″	6″	8″	10″	12″
A	4 ☐	4 ☐	1½	2	2½	3	3½
B	1 ☐	4 ⊠	3¼	4¼	5¼	6¼	7¼
C	4 ◼	8 ◣	1⅞	2⅜	2⅞	3⅜	3⅞
D	4 ☐	4 ☐	1	1¼	1½	1¾	2
E	1 ☐	4 ⊠	2¼	2¾	3¼	3¾	4¼
F	4 ◼	8 ◣	1⅜	1⅝	1⅞	2⅛	2⅜
G	1 ◼	1 ◼	1½	2	2½	3	3½

DESIGN OPTIONS

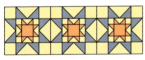

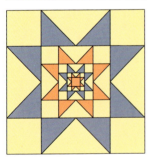

YARDAGE FOR WALL HANGING

16″ × 16″

4″ and 16″ blocks

2 blocks

A, B, D, E: ⅓ yard

C: ¼ yard

F, G: ¼ yard

CUTTING

A, B, D, E (4″, 16″): Cut 1 strip 9¼″ × WOF; subcut into 1 square 9¼″ × 9¼″ (B-16″), 4 squares 4½″ × 4½″ (A-16″), 1 square 5¼″ × 5¼″ (E-16″), 1 square 3¼″ × 3¼″ (B-4″), 4 squares 2½″ × 2½″ (D-16″), 1 square 2¼″ × 2¼″ (E-4″), 4 squares 1½″ × 1½″ (A-4″), and 4 squares 1″ × 1″ (D-4″).

C (4″, 16″): Cut 1 strip 4⅞″ × WOF; subcut into 4 squares 4⅞″ × 4⅞″ (16″) and 4 squares 1⅞″ × 1⅞″ (4″).

F (4″, 16″), G (4″): Cut 1 strip 2⅞″ × WOF; subcut into 4 squares 2⅞″ × 2⅞″ (F-16″), 1 square 1½″ × 1½″ (G-4″), and 4 squares 1⅜″ × 1⅜″ (F-4″).

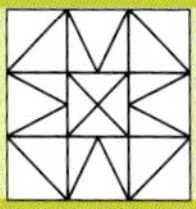

Double Z — 28

 3-GRID

 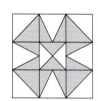

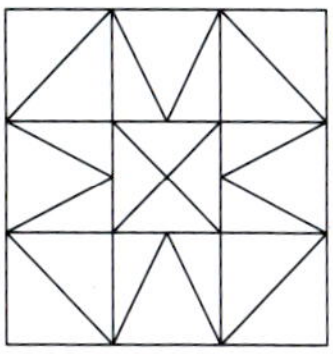

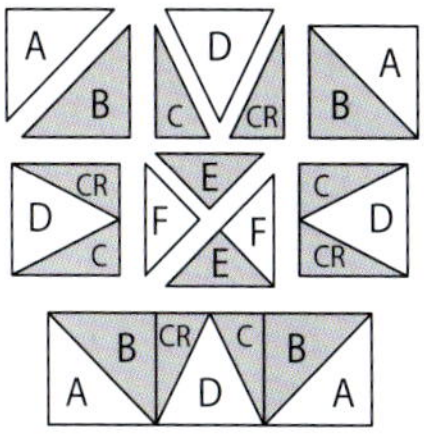

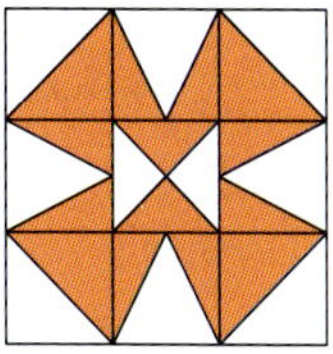

FOR	CUT	NEED	3"	6"	9"	12"	15"
A	2 ☐	4 ◿	1⅞	2⅞	3⅞	4⅞	5⅞
B	2 ☐	4 ◿	1⅞	2⅞	3⅞	4⅞	5⅞
C*	2 ▭	4 ◸	1½ × 1¾	2¼ × 2½	2¾ × 3½	3¼ × 4½	3¾ × 5½
CR*	2 ▭	4 ◹	1½ × 1¾	2¼ × 2½	2¾ × 3½	3¼ × 4½	3¾ × 5½
D*	4 ▭	4 △	1½ × 1⅞	2½ × 2⅞	3½ × 3⅞	4½ × 4⅞	5½ × 5⅞
E	1 ☐	2 ⊠	2¼	3¼	4¼	5¼	6¼
F	1 ☐	2 ⊠	2¼	3¼	4¼	5¼	6¼

Refer to Triangle in a Square (page 122).

DESIGN OPTIONS

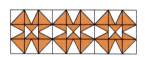

PRECUT FRIENDLY!

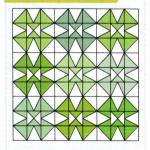

Each 12" block uses:

FQ × ⅔ fat quarter for B, C, CR, E

YARDAGE FOR TWIN QUILT

72" × 96"

12" block

6 × 8 setting = 48 blocks

A, D, F: 5¼ yard

B, C, CR, E: 24 fat quarters

CUTTING

A: Cut 12 strips 4⅞" × WOF; subcut into 96 squares 4⅞" × 4⅞".

D: Cut 24 strips 4½" × WOF; subcut into 192 rectangles 4½" × 4⅞".

F: Cut 3 strips 5¼" × WOF; subcut into 24 squares 5¼" × 5¼".

B, C, CR, E: From each fat quarter, cut 1 strip 5¼" × WOFQ; subcut 1 square 5¼" × 5¼" (E). Cut 1 strip 4⅞" × WOFQ; subcut 4 squares 4⅞" × 4⅞" (B). Cut 2 strips 3¼" × WOFQ; subcut 8 rectangles 3¼" × 4½" (4C, 4CR).

110 Blocks

29 Eccentric Star

3-GRID

 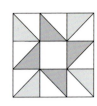 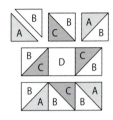 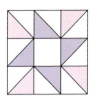

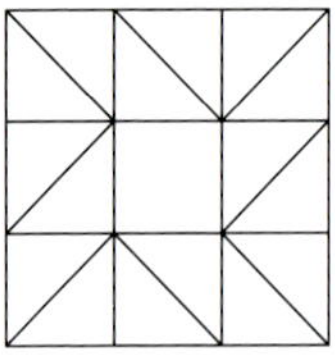

FOR	CUT	NEED	3″	6″	9″	12″	15″
A	2 ☐	4 ◩	1⅞	2⅞	3⅞	4⅞	5⅞
B	4 ☐	8 ◩	1⅞	2⅞	3⅞	4⅞	5⅞
C	2 ▨	4 ◩	1⅞	2⅞	3⅞	4⅞	5⅞
D	1 ☐	1 ☐	1½	2½	3½	4½	5½

DESIGN OPTIONS

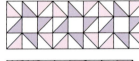

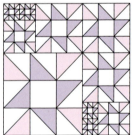

YARDAGE FOR BABY QUILT

48″ × 48″

3″, 6″, 9″, and 15″ blocks

16 × 3″ + 8 × 6″ + 12 × 9″ + 4 × 15″ = 40 blocks

A: 1 yard
B, D: 1⅝ yards
C: 1 yard

CUTTING

NOTE *Make 4 sections as shown then sew the 4 sections together as you wish.*

A (6″, 15″): Cut 2 strips 5⅞″ × WOF; subcut into 8 squares 5⅞″ × 5⅞″ (15″) and 16 squares 2⅞″ × 2⅞″ (6″).

A, 9″: Cut 3 strips 3⅞″ × WOF; subcut into 24 squares 3⅞″ × 3⅞″.

A, 3″: Cut 2 strips 1⅞″ × WOF; subcut into 32 squares 1⅞″ × 1⅞″.

B (6″, 15″): Cut 3 strips 5⅞″ × WOF; subcut into 16 squares 5⅞″ × 5⅞″ (15″) and 20 squares 2⅞″ × 2⅞″ (6″).

B, 9″: Cut 5 strips 3⅞″ × WOF; subcut into 48 squares 3⅞″ × 3⅞″.

B, 6″: Cut 1 strip 2⅞″ × WOF; subcut into 12 squares 2⅞″ × 2⅞″.

B, 3″: Cut 3 strips 1⅞″ × WOF; subcut into 64 squares 1⅞″ × 1⅞″.

D (3″, 6″, 15″): Cut 1 strip 5½″ × WOF; subcut into 4 squares 5½″ × 5½″ (15″), 8 squares 2½″ × 2½″ (6″), and 16 squares 1½″ × 1½″ (3″).

D, 9″: Cut 1 strip 3½″ × WOF; subcut into 12 squares 3½″ × 3½″.

C (6″, 15″): Cut 2 strips 5⅞″ × WOF; subcut into 8 squares 5⅞″ × 5⅞″ (15″) and 16 squares 2⅞″ × 2⅞″ (6″).

C, 9″: Cut 3 strips 3⅞″ × WOF; subcut into 24 squares 3⅞″ × 3⅞″.

C, 3″: Cut 2 strips 1⅞″ × WOF; subcut into 32 squares 1⅞″ × 1⅞″.

Emerald and Topaz 30

6-GRID

  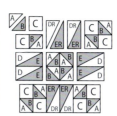 

FOR	CUT	NEED	3″	6″	9″	12″	15″
A	6	12	1 3/8	1 7/8	2 3/8	2 7/8	3 3/8
B	6	12	1 3/8	1 7/8	2 3/8	2 7/8	3 3/8
C	8	8	1	1 1/2	2	2 1/2	3
D	2	4	1 1/4 × 2 1/4	1 3/4 × 3 1/4	2 1/4 × 4 1/4	2 3/4 × 5 1/4	3 1/4 × 6 1/4
DR	2	4	1 1/4 × 2 1/4	1 3/4 × 3 1/4	2 1/4 × 4 1/4	2 3/4 × 5 1/4	3 1/4 × 6 1/4
E	2	4	1 1/4 × 2 1/4	1 3/4 × 3 1/4	2 1/4 × 4 1/4	2 3/4 × 5 1/4	3 1/4 × 6 1/4
ER	2	4	1 1/4 × 2 1/4	1 3/4 × 3 1/4	2 1/4 × 4 1/4	2 3/4 × 5 1/4	3 1/4 × 6 1/4

DESIGN OPTIONS

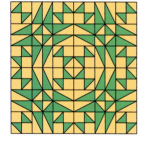

YARDAGE FOR WALL HANGING

30″ × 30″

15″ block

2 × 2 setting = 4 blocks

A, C, D, DR: 7/8 yard

B, E, ER: 5/8 yard

CUTTING

A: Cut 2 strips 3 3/8″ × WOF; subcut into 24 squares 3 3/8″ × 3 3/8″.

C: Cut 3 strips 3″ × WOF; subcut into 32 squares 3″ × 3″.

D, DR: Cut 3 strips 3 1/4″ × WOF; subcut into 16 rectangles 3 1/4″ × 6 1/4″ (8D, 8DR).

B: Cut 2 strips 3 3/8″ × WOF; subcut into 24 squares 3 3/8″ × 3 3/8″.

E, ER: Cut 3 strips 3 1/4″ × WOF; subcut into 16 rectangles 3 1/4″ × 6 1/4″ (8E, 8ER).

31 ▶ Father's Choice

 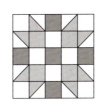 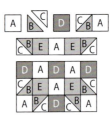 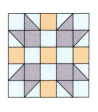

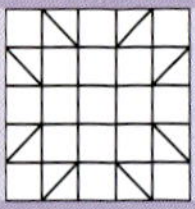

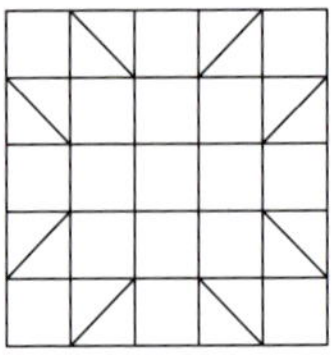

FOR	CUT	NEED	5″	7½″	10″	12½″	15″
A	8 ☐	8 ☐	1½	2	2½	3	3½
B	4 ☐	8 ◪	1⅞	2⅜	2⅞	3⅜	3⅞
C	4 ☐	8 ◪	1⅞	2⅜	2⅞	3⅜	3⅞
D	5 ☐	5 ☐	1½	2	2½	3	3½
E	4 ☐	4 ☐	1½	2	2½	3	3½

DESIGN OPTIONS

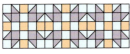

YARDAGE FOR TABLE TOPPER

35⅜″ × 35⅜″

12½″ block

2 × 2 diagonal setting = 4 blocks

A, C, corner triangles: 1⅛ yards

B, E: ½ yard

D: ¼ yard

CUTTING

NOTE *Refer to Side and Corner Triangles for Diagonal Settings (page 127).*

A: Cut 3 strips 3″ × WOF; subcut into 32 squares 3″ × 3″.

C: Cut 2 strips 3⅜″ × WOF; subcut into 16 squares 3⅜″ × 3⅜″.

Corner triangles: Cut 1 strip 18⅝″ × WOF; subcut into 2 squares 18⅝″ × 18⅝″.

B: Cut 2 strips 3⅜″ × WOF; subcut into 16 squares 3⅜″ × 3⅜″.

E: Cut 2 strips 3″ × WOF; subcut into 16 squares 3″ × 3″.

D: Cut 2 strips 3″ × WOF; subcut into 20 squares 3″ × 3″.

Flying Kite — 32

2-GRID

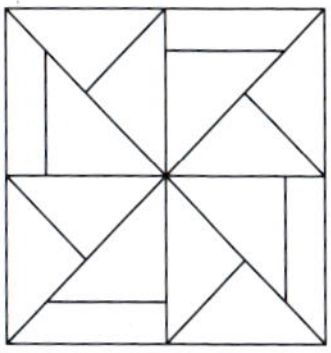

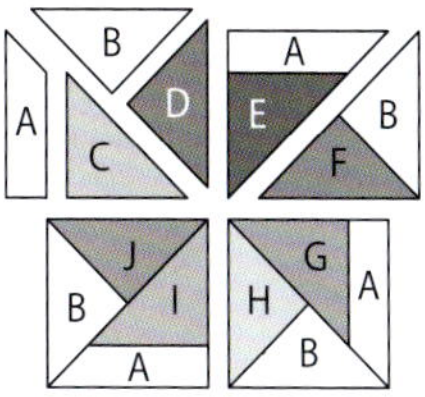

FOR	CUT	NEED	4″	6″	8″	10″	12″
A*	4	4	1 × 2⅞	1¼ × 3⅞	1½ × 4⅞	1¾ × 5⅞	2 × 6⅞
B	1	4	3¼	4¼	5¼	6¼	7¼
C	1	1	2⅜	3⅛	3⅞	4⅝	5⅜
D	1	1	3¼	4¼	5¼	6¼	7¼
E	1	1	2⅜	3⅛	3⅞	4⅝	5⅜
F	1	1	3¼	4¼	5¼	6¼	7¼
G	1	1	2⅜	3⅛	3⅞	4⅝	5⅜
H	1	1	3¼	4¼	5¼	6¼	7¼
I	1	1	2⅜	3⅛	3⅞	4⅝	5⅜
J	1	1	3¼	4¼	5¼	6¼	7¼

Refer to Easy-Cut 45° Angles (page 126).

DESIGN OPTIONS

PRECUT FRIENDLY!

Each 12″ block uses:

LC × 2 squares for C, E, G, I

LC × 1 square for D, F, H, J

YARDAGE FOR BABY QUILT

48″ × 48″

12″ block

4 × 4 setting = 16 blocks

A, B: 1⅝ yards

C, D, E, F, G, H, I, J: 48 layer cake squares

CUTTING

A: Cut 11 strips 2″ × WOF; subcut into 64 rectangles 2″ × 6⅞″.

B: Cut 4 strips 7¼″ × WOF; subcut into 16 squares 7¼″ × 7¼″.

C, E, G, I: Trim 32 layer cake squares to 5⅜″ × 5⅜″.

D, F, H, J: Trim 16 layer cake squares to 7¼″ × 7¼″.

33 Formal Garden

 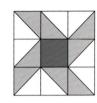 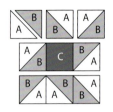 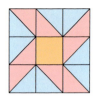

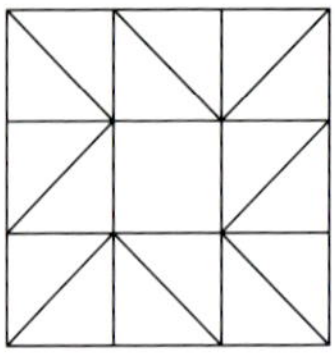

FOR	CUT	NEED	3"	6"	9"	12"	15"
A	4 ☐	8 ◺	1⅞	2⅞	3⅞	4⅞	5⅞
B	4 ☐	8 ◺	1⅞	2⅞	3⅞	4⅞	5⅞
C	1 ☐	1 ☐	1½	2½	3½	4½	5½

DESIGN OPTIONS

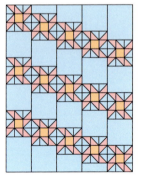

YARDAGE FOR LAP QUILT

60″ × 76″

12″ block

15 blocks plus background blocks

A, background: 3¼ yards

B: 1¼ yards

C: ⅜ yard

CUTTING

A: Cut 7 strips 4⅞″ × WOF; 56 squares 4⅞″ × 4⅞″.

A, background: Cut 6 strips 12½″ × WOF; subcut into 2 rectangles 12½″ × 16½″, 2 rectangles 12½″ × 4½″, 12 squares 12½″ × 12½″, 2 rectangles 12½″ × 8½″, and 4 squares 4⅞″ × 4⅞″.

B: Cut 8 strips 4⅞″ × WOF; 60 squares 4⅞″ × 4⅞″.

C: Cut 2 strips 4½″ × WOF; 15 squares 4½″ × 4½″.

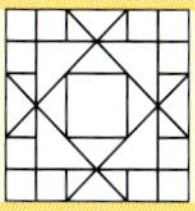

Four Crowns   34

 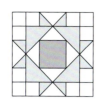 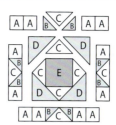 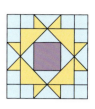

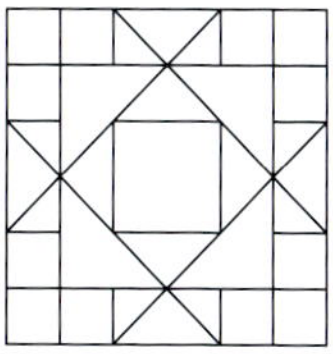

FOR	CUT	NEED	3″	6″	9″	12″	15″
A	12 ☐	12 ☐	1	1½	2	2½	3
B	4 ☐	8 ◺	1⅜	1⅞	2⅜	2⅞	3⅜
C	2 ☐	8 ⊠	2¼	3¼	4¼	5¼	6¼
D	2 ☐	4 ◺	1⅞	2⅞	3⅞	4⅞	5⅞
E	1 ☐	1 ☐	1½	2½	3½	4½	5½

DESIGN OPTIONS

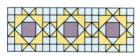

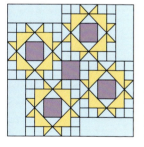

YARDAGE FOR TABLE TOPPER

28″ × 28″

12″ block

4 blocks plus background blocks

A, C, background: ¾ yard

B, D: ⅜ yard

E, center: ¼ yard

CUTTING

NOTE *Quilt is assembled in sections with partial seams. Sew 4 blocks with background rectangles, then sew together with the center square. Refer to Sewing Partial Seams (page 123).*

A: Cut 3 strips 2½″ × WOF; subcut into 48 squares 2½″ × 2½″.

C: Cut 1 strip 5¼″ × WOF; subcut into 8 squares 5¼″ × 5¼″.

Background: Cut 2 strips 4½″ × WOF; subcut into 4 rectangles 4½″ × 12½″.

B: Cut 2 strips 2⅞″ × WOF; subcut into 16 squares 2⅞″ × 2⅞″.

D: Cut 1 strip 4⅞″ × WOF; subcut into 8 squares 4⅞″ × 4⅞″.

E: Cut 1 strip 4½″ × WOF; subcut into 5 squares 4½″ × 4½″ (4E, 1 center).

35 Free Trade

4-GRID

 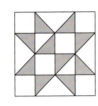 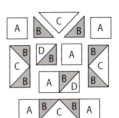 

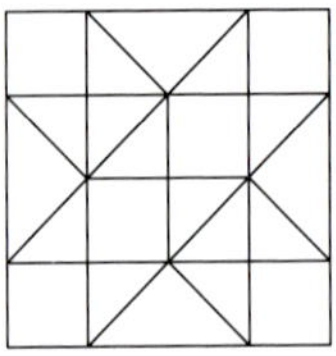

FOR	CUT	NEED	4″	6″	8″	10″	12″
A	6 ▢	6 ▢	1½	2	2½	3	3½
B	5 ◩	10 ◨	1⅞	2⅜	2⅞	3⅜	3⅞
C	1 ▢	4 ⊠	3¼	4¼	5¼	6¼	7¼
D	1 ▢	2 ⊠	1⅞	2⅜	2⅞	3⅜	3⅞

DESIGN OPTIONS

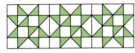

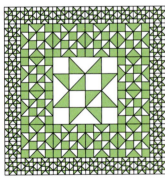

YARDAGE FOR LAP QUILT

60″ × 60″

6″, 12″, 24″ blocks

36 × 6″ + 12 × 12″ + 1 × 24″ = 49 blocks

Fabric 1: 2⅝ yards

Fabric 2: 2⅝ yards

CUTTING

Fabric 1:

A, 24″: Cut 1 strip 6½″ × WOF; subcut into 6 squares 6½″ × 6½″.

A, 6″: Cut 11 strips 2″ × WOF; subcut into 216 squares 2″ × 2″.

B, 12″: Cut 6 strips 3⅞″ × WOF; subcut into 60 squares 3⅞″ × 3⅞″.

C (24″), D (6″, 24″): Cut 1 strip 13¼″ × WOF; subcut into 1 square 13¼″ × 13¼″ (C), 1 square 6⅞″ × 6⅞″ (D-24″), and 2 squares 2⅜″ × 2⅜″ (D-6″).

C, 6″: Cut 4 strips 4¼″ × WOF; subcut into 36 squares 4¼″ × 4¼″.

D, 6″: Cut 2 strips 2⅜″ × WOF; subcut into 34 squares 2⅜″ × 2⅜″.

Fabric 2:

A, 12″: Cut 6 strips 3½″ × WOF; subcut into 72 squares 3½″ × 3½″.

B, 24″: Cut 1 strip 6⅞″ × WOF; subcut into 5 squares 6⅞″ × 6⅞″.

B, 6″: Cut 11 strips 2⅜″ × WOF; subcut into 180 squares 2⅜″ × 2⅜″.

C, 12″: Cut 3 strips 7¼″ × WOF; subcut into 12 squares 7¼″ × 7¼″.

D, 12″: Cut 2 strips 3⅞″ × WOF; subcut into 12 squares 3⅞″ × 3⅞″.

Friendship Block   36

6-GRID

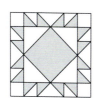

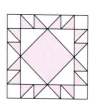

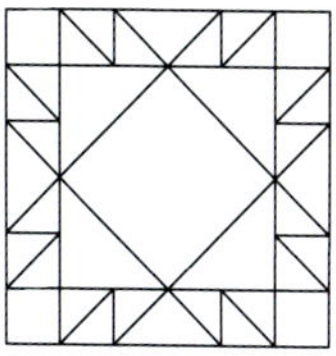

FOR	CUT	NEED	3″	6″	9″	12″	15″
A	4 ☐	4 ☐	1	1½	2	2½	3
B	8 ◩	16 ◸	1⅜	1⅞	2⅜	2⅞	3⅜
C	4 ☐	8 ◸	1⅜	1⅞	2⅜	2⅞	3⅜
D	1 ☐	4 ⊠	2¼	3¼	4¼	5¼	6¼
E	2 ☐	4 ◹	1⅞	2⅞	3⅞	4⅞	5⅞
F	1 ◩	1 ◩	1⅞	3⅜	4¾	6⅛	7⅝

DESIGN OPTIONS

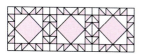

PRECUT FRIENDLY!

Each 9″ block uses:

CS ×1 square for F

YARDAGE FOR LAP QUILT

63″ × 63″

9″ block

7 × 7 setting = 49 blocks

A, C, D, E: 3¼ yards

B: 1¾ yards

F: 49 charm squares

CUTTING

A: Cut 10 strips 2″ × WOF; subcut into 196 squares 2″ × 2″.

C: Cut 12 strips 2⅜″ × WOF; subcut into 196 squares 2⅜″ × 2⅜″.

D: Cut 6 strips 4¼″ × WOF; subcut into 49 squares 4¼″ × 4¼″.

E: Cut 10 strips 3⅞″ × WOF; subcut into 98 squares 3⅞″ × 3⅞″.

B: Cut 24 strips 2⅜″ × WOF; subcut into 392 squares 2⅜″ × 2⅜″.

F: Trim each charm square to 4¾″ × 4¾″.

37 Friendship Star

3-GRID

  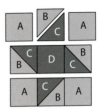 

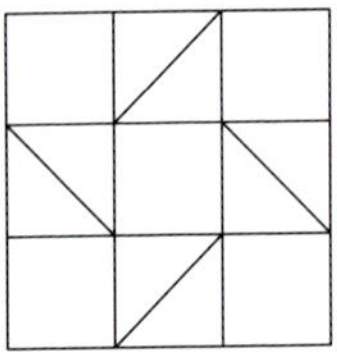

FOR	CUT	NEED	3"	6"	9"	12"	15"
A	4	4	1½	2½	3½	4½	5½
B	2	4	1⅞	2⅞	3⅞	4⅞	5⅞
C	2	4	1⅞	2⅞	3⅞	4⅞	5⅞
D	1	1	1½	2½	3½	4½	5½

DESIGN OPTIONS

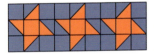

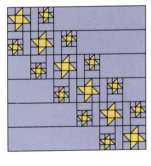

YARDAGE FOR BABY QUILT

54″ × 54″

6″ and 9″ blocks

16 blocks plus background blocks

A, B, background: 2⅞ yards

C, D: ¾ yard

CUTTING

A, 9″: Cut 2 strips 3½″ × WOF; subcut into 24 squares 3½″ × 3½″.

A, 6″: Cut 3 strips 2½″ × WOF; subcut into 40 squares 2½″ × 2½″.

B, 9″: Cut 2 strips 3⅞″ × WOF; subcut into 12 squares 3⅞″ × 3⅞″.

B, 6″: Cut 2 strips 2⅞″ × WOF; subcut into 20 squares 2⅞″ × 2⅞″.

Background: Cut 6 strips 9½″ × WOF; subcut into 2 rectangles 9½″ × 36½″, 2 rectangles 9½″ × 27½″, 2 rectangles 9½″ × 18½″, 2 squares 9½″ × 9½″, 10 rectangles 9½″ × 3½″. Cut 1 strip 6½″ × WOF; subcut into 10 rectangles 6½″ × 3½″.

C, 9″: Cut 2 strips 3⅞″ × WOF; subcut into 12 squares 3⅞″ × 3⅞″.

C, 6″: Cut 2 strips 2⅞″ × WOF; subcut into 20 squares 2⅞″ × 2⅞″.

D, 9″: Cut 1 strip 3½″ × WOF; subcut into 6 squares 3½″ × 3½″.

D, 6″: Cut 1 strip 2½″ × WOF; subcut into 10 squares 2½″ × 2½″.

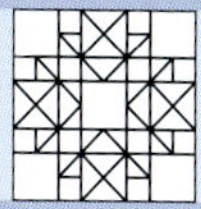

Green Mountain Star 38

8-GRID

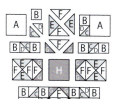
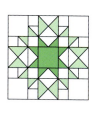

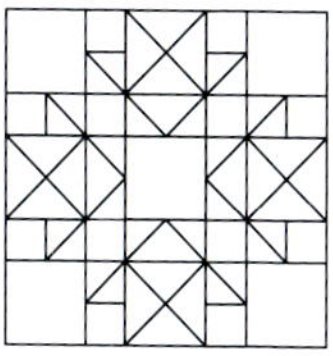

FOR	CUT	NEED	4″	6″	8″	10″	12″
A	4	4	1½	2	2½	3	3½
B	12	12	1	1¼	1½	1¾	2
C	4	8	1⅜	1⅝	1⅞	2⅛	2⅜
D	4	8	1⅜	1⅝	1⅞	2⅛	2⅜
E	2	8	2¼	2¾	3¼	3¾	4¼
F	3	12	2¼	2¾	3¼	3¾	4¼
G	4	8	1⅜	1⅝	1⅞	2⅛	2⅜
H	1	1	1½	2	2½	3	3½

DESIGN OPTIONS

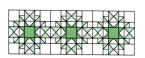

PRECUT FRIENDLY!

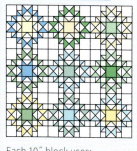

Each 10″ block uses:

LC × ½ square for C, E

LC × ⅓ square for G, H

YARDAGE FOR LAP QUILT

60″ × 60″

10″ block

6 × 6 setting = 36 blocks

A, B, D, F: 3⅝ yards

C, E, G, H: 36 layer cake squares

CUTTING

NOTE *Mix and match sets of 4C and 2E with sets of 4G and H.*

A: Cut 11 strips 3″ × WOF; subcut into 144 squares 3″ × 3″.

B: Cut 18 strips 1¾″ × WOF; subcut into 432 squares 1¾″ × 1¾″.

D: Cut 8 strips 2⅛″ × WOF; subcut into 144 squares 2⅛″ × 2⅛″.

F: Cut 10 strips 3¾″ × WOF; subcut into 108 squares 3¾″ × 3¾″.

C, E, G, H: From each layer cake square, cut 1 strip 3¾″ × 10″; subcut 2 squares 3¾″ × 3¾″ (E) and 1 square 2⅛″ × 2⅛″ (1C); cut 1 strip 3″ × 10″; subcut 1 square 3″ × 3″ (H) and 3 squares 2⅛″ × 2⅛″ (3C) ; cut 1 strip 2⅛″ × 10″; subcut 4 squares 2⅛″ × 2⅛″ (4G).

39 Halley's Comet

5-GRID

 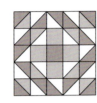 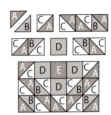 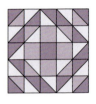

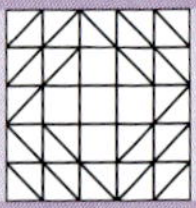

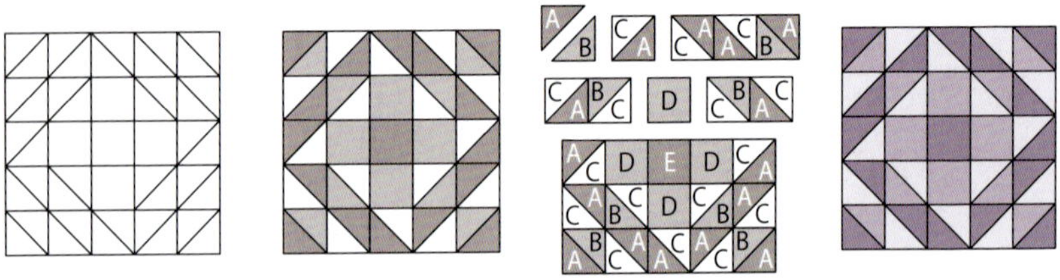

FOR	CUT	NEED	5″	7½″	10″	12½″	15″
A	8	16	1⅞	2⅜	2⅞	3⅜	3⅞
B	4	8	1⅞	2⅜	2⅞	3⅜	3⅞
C	8	16	1⅞	2⅜	2⅞	3⅜	3⅞
D	4	4	1½	2	2½	3	3½
E	1	1	1½	2	2½	3	3½

DESIGN OPTIONS

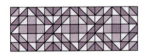

PRECUT FRIENDLY!

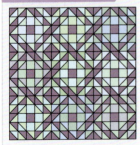

Each 7½″ block uses:

Jelly roll × ½ strip for B, D
Jelly roll × ½ strip for C

YARDAGE FOR BABY QUILT

45″ × 45″

7½″ block

6 × 6 setting = 36 blocks

A, E: 1⅜ yards

B, C, D: 36 jelly roll strips

CUTTING

A: Cut 17 strips 2⅜″ × WOF; subcut into 288 squares 2⅜″ × 2⅜″.

E: Cut 2 strips 2″ × WOF; subcut into 36 squares 2″ × 2″.

B, C, D: From each jelly roll strip, cut 12 squares 2⅜″ × 2⅜″ (4B, 8C) and 4 squares 2″ × 2″ (D).

5-GRID | Hope of Hartford | 40

  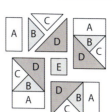 

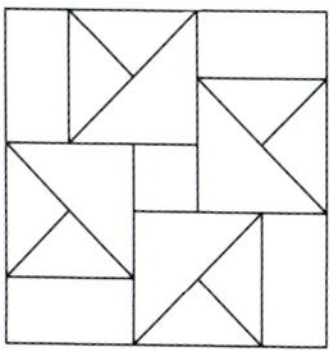

FOR	CUT	NEED	5"	7½"	10"	12½"	15"
A	4	4	1½ × 2½	2 × 3½	2½ × 4½	3 × 5½	3½ × 6½
B	1	4	3¼	4¼	5¼	6¼	7¼
C	1	4	3¼	4¼	5¼	6¼	7¼
D*	2	4	2⅞	3⅞	4⅞	5⅞	6⅞
E*	1	1	1½	2	2½	3	3½

* *Refer to Sewing Partial Seams (page 123).*

DESIGN OPTIONS

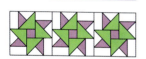

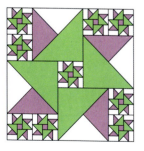

YARDAGE FOR LAP QUILT

50" × 50"

10" block

9 blocks and pieced background

A, C, background: 1⅛ yards

B, E, background: ¾ yard

D, background: 1¼ yards

CUTTING

A, background: Cut 1 strip 21¼" × WOF; subcut into 1 square 21¼" × 21¼", cut in half diagonally twice (background), 32 rectangles 2½" × 4½" (A).

A, C: Cut 2 strips 5¼" × WOF; subcut into 9 squares 5¼" × 5¼" (C), 4 rectangles 2½" × 4½" (A).

B, E, background: Cut 1 strip 21¼" × WOF; subcut into 1 square 21¼" × 21¼", cut in half diagonally twice (background), 9 squares 5¼" × 5¼" (B), and 9 squares 2½" × 2½" (E).

D: Cut 3 strips 4⅞" × WOF; subcut into 18 squares 4⅞" × 4⅞".

Background: Cut 1 strip 20⅞" × WOF; subcut into 2 squares 20⅞" × 20⅞", cut in half diagonally.

41 Illinois Star

6-GRID

 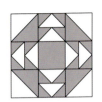 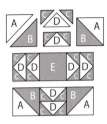 

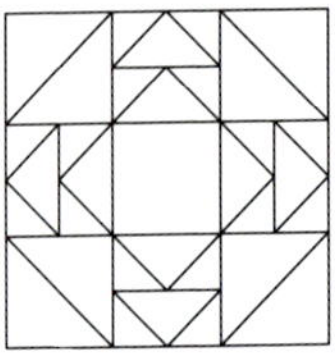

FOR	CUT	NEED	3″	6″	9″	12″	15″
A	2 □	4 ◩	1⅞	2⅞	3⅞	4⅞	5⅞
B	2 ■	4 ◩	1⅞	2⅞	3⅞	4⅞	5⅞
C	8 ■	16 ◩	1⅜	1⅞	2⅜	2⅞	3⅜
D	2 □	8 ⊠	2¼	3¼	4¼	5¼	6¼
E	1 ■	1 ■	1½	2½	3½	4½	5½

DESIGN OPTIONS

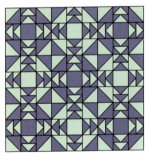

YARDAGE FOR DOUBLE QUILT

75″ × 90″

15″ block

5 × 6 setting = 30 blocks

Fabric 1: 4 yards
Fabric 2: 4 yards

CUTTING

From each fabric:

A: Cut 5 strips 5⅞″ × WOF; subcut into 30 squares 5⅞″ × 5⅞″.

B, E: Cut 5 strips 5⅞″ × WOF; subcut into 30 squares 5⅞″ × 5⅞″ (B) and 1 square 5½″ × 5½″ (E).

C: Cut 10 strips 3⅜″ × WOF; subcut into 120 squares 3⅜″ × 3⅜″.

D: Cut 5 strips 6¼″ × WOF; subcut into 30 squares 6¼″ × 6¼″.

E: Cut 2 strips 5½″ × WOF; subcut into 14 squares 5½″ × 5½″.

4-GRID

Judy's Star — 42

 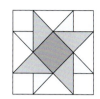 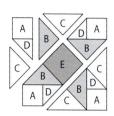 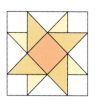

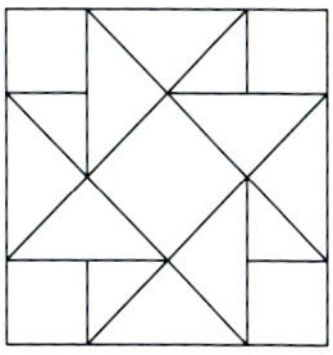

FOR	CUT	NEED	4"	6"	8"	10"	12"
A	4	4	1½	2	2½	3	3½
B	1	4	3¼	4¼	5¼	6¼	7¼
C	1	4	3¼	4¼	5¼	6¼	7¼
D	2	4	1⅞	2⅜	2⅞	3⅜	3⅞
E	1	1	1⅞	2⅝	3⅜	4	4¾

DESIGN OPTIONS

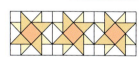

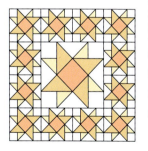

YARDAGE FOR BABY QUILT

48″ × 48″

12″ and 24″ blocks

12 × 12″ + 1 × 24″ = 13 blocks

A, C: 1⅜ yards

B: ⅞ yard

D: ⅝ yard

E: ⅝ yard

CUTTING

A (24″), C (12″, 24″): Cut 1 strip 13¼″ × WOF; subcut into 1 square 13¼″ × 13¼″ (C-24), 2 squares 7¼″ × 7¼″ (C-12″), and 4 squares 6½″ × 6½″ (A).

A, 12″: Cut 4 strips 3½″ × WOF; subcut into 48 squares 3½″ × 3½″.

C, 12″: Cut 2 strips 7¼″ × WOF; subcut into 10 squares 7¼″ × 7¼″.

B (24″, 12″): Cut 1 strip 13¼″ × WOF; subcut into 1 square 13¼″ × 13¼″ (24″), 2 squares 7¼″ × 7¼″ (12″).

B, 12″: Cut 2 strips 7¼″ × WOF; subcut into 10 squares 7¼″ × 7¼″.

D (24″, 12″): Cut 1 strip 6⅞″ × WOF; subcut into 2 squares 6⅞″ × 6⅞″ (24″) and 4 squares 3⅞″ × 3⅞″ (12″).

D, 12″: Cut 2 strips 3⅞″ × WOF; subcut into 20 squares 3⅞″ × 3⅞″.

E (24″, 12″): Cut 1 strip 9″ × WOF; subcut into 1 square 9″ × 9″ (24″) and 4 squares 4¾″ × 4¾″ (12″).

E, 12″: Cut 1 strip 4¾″ × WOF; subcut into 8 squares 4¾″ × 4¾″.

43 King's Crown

 6-GRID

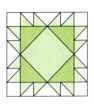

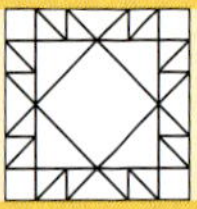

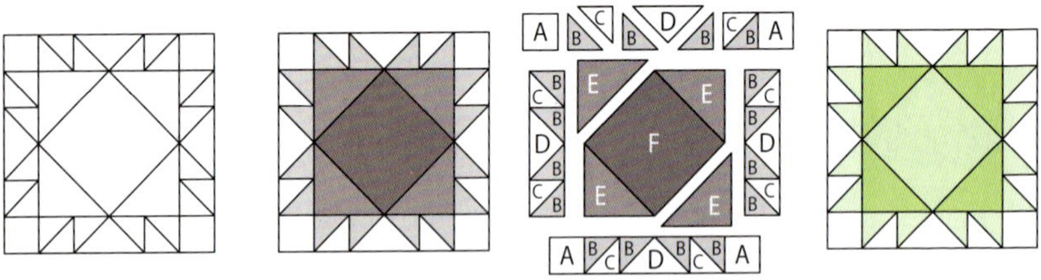

FOR	CUT	NEED	3"	6"	9"	12"	15"
A	4	4	1	1½	2	2½	3
B	8	16	1⅜	1⅞	2⅜	2⅞	3⅜
C	4	8	1⅜	1⅞	2⅜	2⅞	3⅜
D	1	4	2¼	3¼	4¼	5¼	6¼
E	2	4	1⅞	2⅞	3⅞	4⅞	5⅞
F	1	1	1⅞	3⅜	4¾	6⅛	7⅝

DESIGN OPTIONS

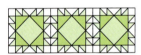

PRECUT FRIENDLY!

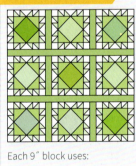

Each 9″ block uses:

CS × 1 square for F

YARDAGE FOR BABY QUILT

61½″ × 61½″

9″ block

6 × 6 setting = 36 blocks

A, C, D: 1⅝ yards

B: 1¼ yards

E: 1 yard

F: 36 charm squares

Sashing: 1 yard

CUTTING

A: Cut 7 strips 2″ × WOF; subcut into 144 squares 2″ × 2″.

C: Cut 9 strips 2⅜″ × WOF; subcut into 144 squares 2⅜″ × 2⅜″.

D: Cut 4 strips 4¼″ × WOF; subcut into 36 squares 4¼″ × 4¼″.

B: Cut 17 strips 2⅜″ × WOF; subcut into 288 squares 2⅜″ × 2⅜″.

E: Cut 8 strips 3⅞″ × WOF; subcut into 72 squares 3⅞″ × 3⅞″.

F: Trim charm squares to 4¾″ × 4¾″.

Sashing: Cut 16 strips 2″ × WOF; subcut into 30 rectangles 2″ × 9½″; sew together 8 strips and subcut into 5 strips 2″ × 62″.

4-GRID

Land of Lincoln 44

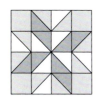
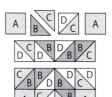
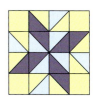

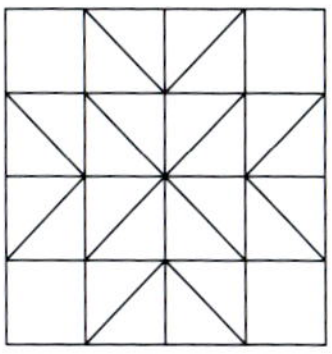

FOR	CUT	NEED	4″	6″	8″	10″	12″
A	4	4	1½	2	2½	3	3½
B	4	8	1⅞	2⅜	2⅞	3⅜	3⅞
C	4	8	1⅞	2⅜	2⅞	3⅜	3⅞
D	4	8	1⅞	2⅜	2⅞	3⅜	3⅞

DESIGN OPTIONS

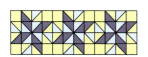

PRECUT FRIENDLY!

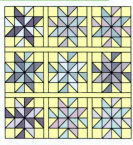

Each 8″ block uses:

LC × ½ square for B

LC × ½ square for D

YARDAGE FOR TWIN QUILT

71″ × 89″

8″ block

8 × 10 setting = 80 blocks

A, C, sashing: 4¼ yards

B, D: 80 layer cake squares

CUTTING

NOTE *Mix and match sets of 4B and 4D for each block.*

A: Cut 20 strips 2½″ × WOF; subcut into 320 squares 2½″ × 2½″.

C: Cut 23 strips 2⅞″ × WOF; subcut into 320 squares 2⅞″ × 2⅞″.

Sashing: Cut 3 strips 8½″ × WOF; subcut into 70 rectangles 1½″ × 8½″. Cut 16 strips 1½″ × WOF; sew together and subcut into 9 strips 1½″ × 71½″.

B, D: Cut each layer cake square into 8 squares 2⅞″ × 2⅞″ (4B, 4D).

110 Blocks

45 Large Star

 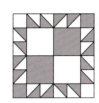 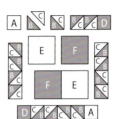

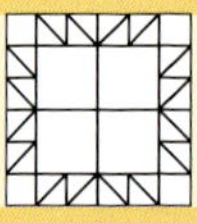

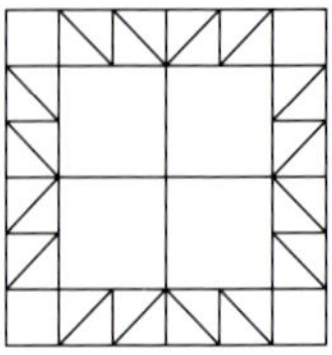

FOR	CUT	NEED	3″	6″	9″	12″	15″
A	2	2	1	1½	2	2½	3
B	8	16	1⅜	1⅞	2⅜	2⅞	3⅜
C	8	16	1⅜	1⅞	2⅜	2⅞	3⅜
D	2	2	1	1½	2	2½	3
E	2	2	1½	2½	3½	4½	5½
F	2	2	1½	2½	3½	4½	5½

DESIGN OPTIONS

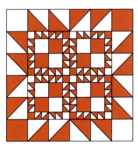

YARDAGE FOR WALL HANGING

36″ × 36″

12″ block

2 × 2 setting = 4 blocks plus pieced border

A, C, E, border: ¾ yard

B, D, F, border: ¾ yard

CUTTING

A, C, border: Cut 2 strips 6⅞″ × WOF; subcut into 8 squares 6⅞″ × 6⅞″ (border), 2 squares 6½″ × 6½″ (border), 4 squares 2⅞″ × 2⅞″ (C), and 6 squares 2½″ × 2½″ (A).

A, E: Cut 1 strip 4½″ × WOF; subcut into 8 squares 4½″ × 4½″ (E) and 2 squares 2½″ × 2½″ (A).

C: Cut 2 strips 2⅞″ × WOF; subcut into 28 squares 2⅞″ × 2⅞″.

B, D, border: Cut 2 strips 6⅞″ × WOF; subcut into 8 squares 6⅞″ × 6⅞″ (border), 2 squares 6½″ × 6½″ (border), 4 squares 2⅞″ × 2⅞″ (B), and 6 squares 2½″ × 2½″ (D).

D, F: Cut 1 strip 4½″ × WOF; subcut into 8 squares 4½″ × 4½″ (F) and 2 squares 2½″ × 2½″ (D).

B: Cut 2 strips 2⅞″ × WOF; subcut into 28 squares 2⅞″ × 2⅞″.

6-GRID

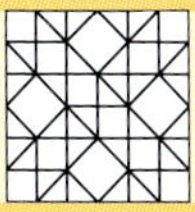

Lover's Lane — 46

  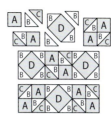 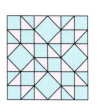

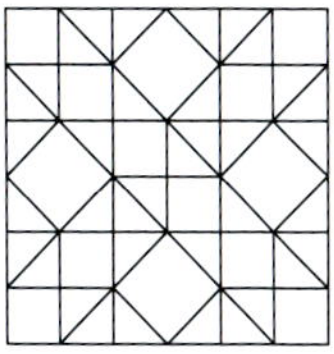

FOR	CUT	NEED	3″	6″	9″	12″	15″
A	10	10	1	1½	2	2½	3
B	13	26	1⅜	1⅞	2⅜	2⅞	3⅜
C	5	10	1⅜	1⅞	2⅜	2⅞	3⅜
D	4	4	1¼	1⅞	2⅝	3⅜	4

DESIGN OPTIONS

YARDAGE FOR WALL HANGING

30″ × 30″

15″ block

2 × 2 setting = 4 blocks

A, C, D: ⅞ yard

B: ⅝ yard

CUTTING

A: Cut 3 strips 3″ × WOF; subcut into 40 squares 3″ × 3″.

C: Cut 2 strips 3⅜″ × WOF; subcut into 20 squares 3⅜″ × 3⅜″.

D: Cut 2 strips 4″ × WOF; subcut into 16 squares 4″ × 4″.

B: Cut 5 strips 3⅜″ × WOF; subcut into 52 squares 3⅜″ × 3⅜″.

110 Blocks

47 Martha Washington Star

  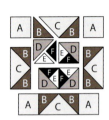 

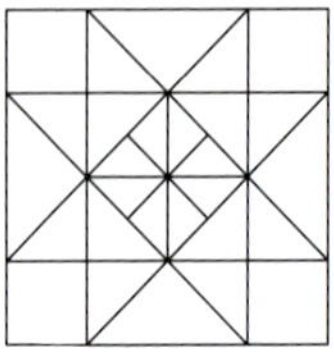

FOR	CUT	NEED	4″	6″	8″	10″	12″
A	4	4	1½	2	2½	3	3½
B	4	8	1⅞	2⅜	2⅞	3⅜	3⅞
C	1	4	3¼	4¼	5¼	6¼	7¼
D	2	4	1⅞	2⅜	2⅞	3⅜	3⅞
E	1	4	2¼	2¾	3¼	3¾	4¼
F	1	4	2¼	2¾	3¼	3¾	4¼

DESIGN OPTIONS

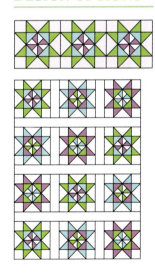

YARDAGE FOR BABY QUILT

40″ × 54″

12″ block

3 × 4 setting = 12 blocks

A, C, E, sashing: 1⅞ yards

B, D, F: ⅝ yard each of 3 fabrics

CUTTING

A: Cut 4 strips 3½″ × WOF; subcut into 48 squares 3½″ × 3½″.

C: Cut 3 strips 7¼″ × WOF; subcut into 12 squares 7¼″ × 7¼″.

E: Cut 2 strips 4¼″ × WOF; subcut into 12 squares 4¼″ × 4¼″.

Sashing: Cut 6 strips 2½″ × WOF; subcut into 3 strips 2½″ × 40½″ and 8 rectangles 2½″ × 12½″.

From each of the 3 fabrics:

B, D: Cut 3 strips 3⅞″ × WOF; subcut into 24 squares 3⅞″ × 3⅞″ (16B, 8D).

F: Cut 1 strip 4¼″ × WOF; subcut into 4 squares 4¼″ × 4¼″.

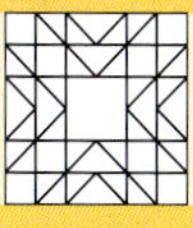

Memory 48

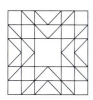 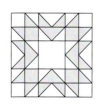 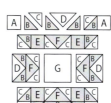 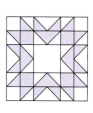

FOR	CUT	NEED	3″	6″	9″	12″	15″
A	4	4	1	1½	2	2½	3
B	8	16	1⅜	1⅞	2⅜	2⅞	3⅜
C	8	16	1⅜	1⅞	2⅜	2⅞	3⅜
D	1	4	2¼	3¼	4¼	5¼	6¼
E	4	4	1	1½	2	2½	3
F	1	4	2¼	3¼	4¼	5¼	6¼
G	1	1	1½	2½	3½	4½	5½

DESIGN OPTIONS

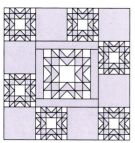

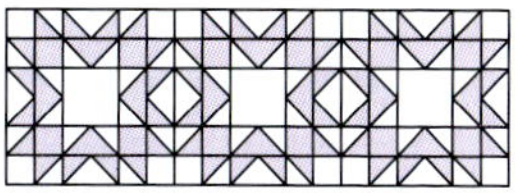

YARDAGE FOR WALL HANGING

24″ × 24″

6″ and 9″ blocks

6 × 6″ + 1 × 9″ = 7 blocks plus 6 alternate blocks

A, C, D, G: ⅝ yard

B, E, F, alternate blocks, sashing: ¾ yard

CUTTING

A (6″, 9″): Cut 1 strip 2″ × WOF; subcut into 4 squares 2″ × 2″ (9″) and 22 squares 1½″ × 1½″ (6″).

A (6″), C (6″, 9″): Cut 1 strip 2⅜″ × WOF; subcut into 8 squares 2⅜″ × 2⅜″ (C-9″) and 4 squares 1⅞″ × 1⅞″ (C-6″), and 2 squares 1½″ × 1½″ (A).

C, 6″: Cut 2 strips 1⅞″ × WOF; subcut into 44 squares 1⅞″ × 1⅞″.

D (6″, 9″): Cut 1 strip 4¼″ × WOF; subcut into 1 square 4¼″ × 4¼″ (9″), 6 squares 3¼″ × 3¼″ (6″).

G (6″, 9″): Cut 1 strip 3½″ × WOF; subcut 1 square 3½″ × 3½″ (9″) and 6 squares 2½″ × 2½″ (6″).

B, 6″: Cut 2 strips 1⅞″ × WOF; subcut into 44 squares 1⅞″ × 1⅞″.

B (6″, 9″), E (6″): Cut 1 strip 2⅜″ × WOF; subcut into 8 squares 2⅜″ × 2⅜″ (B-9″), 4 squares 1⅞″ × 1⅞″ (B-6″), and 2 squares 1½″ × 1½″ (E).

E (6″, 12″): Cut 1 strip 2″ × WOF; subcut into 4 squares 2″ × 2″ (12″) and 22 squares 1½″ × 1½″ (6″).

F (6″, 12″): Cut 1 strip 4¼″ × WOF; subcut into 1 square 4¼″ × 4¼″ (12″), 6 squares 3¼″ × 3¼″ (6″).

Alternate blocks: Cut 1 strip 6½″ × WOF; subcut into 6 squares 6½″ × 6½″.

Sashing: Cut 2 strips 2″ × WOF; subcut into 2 rectangles 2″ × 12½″ and 2 rectangles 2″ × 9½″.

110 Blocks 59

49 Milky Way

 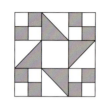 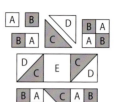

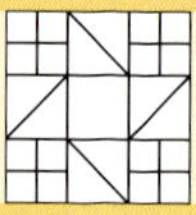

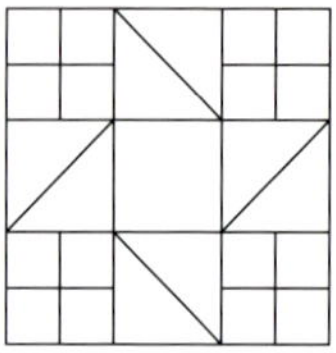

FOR	CUT	NEED	3"	6"	9"	12"	15"
A	8	8	1	1½	2	2½	3
B	8	8	1	1½	2	2½	3
C	2	4	1⅞	2⅞	3⅞	4⅞	5⅞
D	2	4	1⅞	2⅞	3⅞	4⅞	5⅞
E	1	1	1½	2½	3½	4½	5½

DESIGN OPTIONS

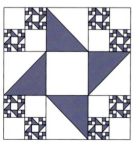

YARDAGE FOR BABY QUILT

36" × 36"

6" block

8 blocks and pieced background

A, D, E, background: 1 yard

B, C, background: ⅝ yard

CUTTING

A: Cut 2 strips 1½" × WOF; subcut into 56 squares 1½" × 1½".

A, E: Cut 1 strip 2½" × WOF; subcut into 8 squares 2½" × 2½" (E) and 8 squares 1½" × 1½" (A).

D, background: Cut 2 strips 6½" × WOF; subcut into 8 squares 6½" × 6½" (background) and 16 squares 2⅞" × 2⅞" (D).

Background: Cut 1 strip 12⅞" × WOF; subcut into 2 squares 12⅞" × 12⅞", cut in half diagonally, and 1 square 12½" × 12½".

B: Cut 3 strips 1½" × WOF; subcut into 64 squares 1½" × 1½".

C, background: Cut 1 strip 12⅞" × WOF; subcut into 2 squares 12⅞" × 12⅞", cut in half diagonally (background), 16 squares 2⅞" × 2⅞" (C).

Missouri Blossom 50

4-GRID

 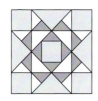 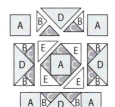 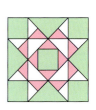

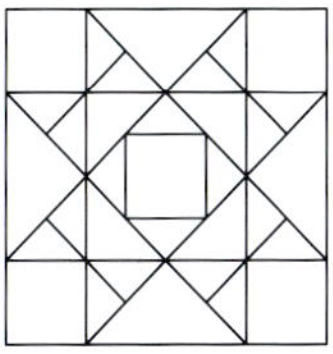

FOR	CUT	NEED	4″	6″	8″	10″	12″
A	5	5	1½	2	2½	3	3½
B	2	8	2¼	2¾	3¼	3¾	4¼
C	3	12	2¼	2¾	3¼	3¾	4¼
D	1	4	3¼	4¼	5¼	6¼	7¼
E	2	4	1⅞	2⅜	2⅞	3⅜	3⅞

DESIGN OPTIONS

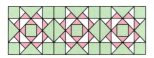

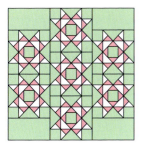

YARDAGE FOR TABLE TOPPER

30″ × 30″

10″ block

7 blocks plus background blocks

A, D, background: ¾ yard

B, E: ½ yard

C: ⅓ yard

CUTTING

A: Cut 1 strip 3″ × WOF; subcut into 14 squares 3″ × 3″.

A, D: Cut 2 strips 6¼″ × WOF; subcut into 7 squares 6¼″ × 6¼″ (D) and 21 squares 3″ × 3″ (A).

Background: Cut 1 strip 5½″ × WOF; subcut into 4 rectangles 5½″ × 10½″.

B, E: Cut 2 strips 3¾″ × WOF; subcut into 14 squares 3¾″ × 3¾″ (B) and 2 squares 3⅜″ × 3⅜″ (E).

E: Cut 1 strip 3⅜″ × WOF; subcut into 12 squares 3⅜″ × 3⅜″.

C: Cut 2 strips 3¾″ × WOF; subcut into 21 squares 3¾″ × 3¾″.

51 Mosaic Star

6-GRID

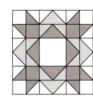
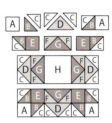
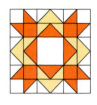

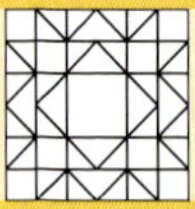

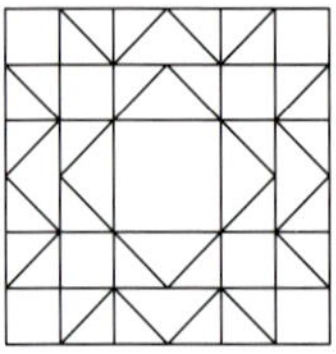

FOR	CUT	NEED	3"	6"	9"	12"	15"
A	4	4	1	1½	2	2½	3
B	4	8	1⅜	1⅞	2⅜	2⅞	3⅜
C	8	16	1⅜	1⅞	2⅜	2⅞	3⅜
D	1	4	2¼	3¼	4¼	5¼	6¼
E	4	4	1	1½	2	2½	3
F	4	8	1⅜	1⅞	2⅜	2⅞	3⅜
G	1	4	2¼	3¼	4¼	5¼	6¼
H	1	1	1½	2½	3½	4½	5½

DESIGN OPTIONS

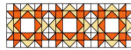
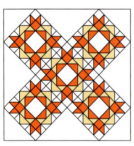

YARDAGE FOR WALL HANGING

42½" × 42½"

15" block

5 blocks

A, C, H, side and corner triangles: 1⅜ yards

B, E, G: ⅝ yard

D, F: ½ yard

CUTTING

NOTE *Refer to Side and Corner Triangles for Diagonal Settings (page 127).*

A, C, side and corner triangles: Cut 1 strip 23" × WOF; subcut into 1 square 22½" × 22½" (side triangles), 2 squares 11½" × 11½", (corner triangles), 4 squares 3⅜" × 3⅜" (C), and 6 squares 3" × 3" (A).

A: Cut 1 strip 3" × WOF; subcut into 14 squares 3" × 3".

C: Cut 3 strips 3⅜" × WOF; subcut into 36 squares 3⅜" × 3⅜".

H: Cut 1 strip 5½" × WOF; subcut into 5 squares 5½" × 5½".

B: Cut 2 strips 3⅜" × WOF; subcut into 20 squares 3⅜" × 3⅜".

E: Cut 2 strips 3" × WOF; subcut into 20 squares 3" × 3".

G: Cut 1 strip 6¼" × WOF; subcut into 5 squares 6¼" × 6¼".

D: Cut 1 strip 6¼" × WOF; subcut into 5 squares 6¼" × 6¼".

F: Cut 2 strips 3⅜" × WOF; subcut into 20 squares 3⅜" × 3⅜".

Quick & Easy All Stars Block Tool

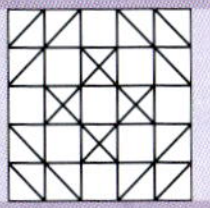

Mrs. Jones' Favorite — 52

5-GRID

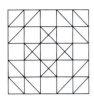
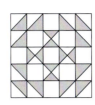
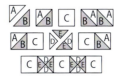
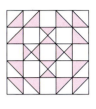

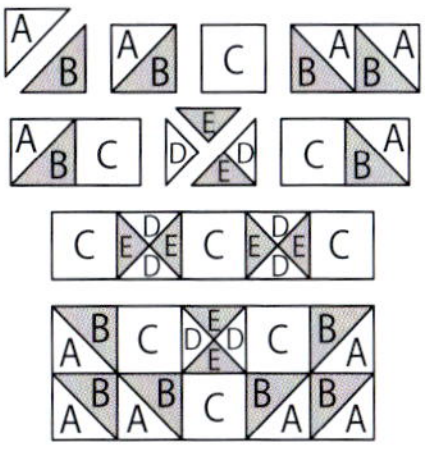

FOR	CUT	NEED	5″	7½″	10″	12½″	15″
A	6	12	1⅞	2⅜	2⅞	3⅜	3⅞
B	6	12	1⅞	2⅜	2⅞	3⅜	3⅞
C	9	9	1½	2	2½	3	3½
D	2	8	2¼	2¾	3¼	3¾	4¼
E	2	8	2¼	2¾	3¼	3¾	4¼

DESIGN OPTIONS

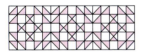

PRECUT FRIENDLY!

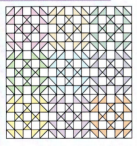

Each 10″ block uses:

LC × 1 square for B, E

YARDAGE FOR LAP QUILT

60″ × 60″

10″ block

6 × 6 setting = 36 blocks

A, C, D: 3½ yards

B, E: 36 layer cake squares

CUTTING

A: Cut 16 strips 2⅞″ × WOF; subcut into 216 squares 2⅞″ × 2⅞″.

C: Cut 21 strips 2½″ × WOF; subcut into 324 squares 2½″ × 2½″.

D: Cut 6 strips 3¼″ × WOF; subcut into 72 squares 3¼″ × 3¼″.

B, E: From each layer cake square, cut 2 squares 3¼″ × 3¼″ (E) and 6 squares 2⅞″ × 2⅞″ (B).

53 Nine-Patch Star

3-GRID

 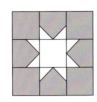 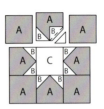 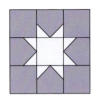

FOR	CUT	NEED	3″	6″	9″	12″	15″
A	8	8	1½	2½	3½	4½	5½
B*	8	8	1	1½	2	2½	3
C	1	1	1½	2½	3½	4½	5½

*Refer to Sewing Squares to Squares or Rectangles (page 123)

DESIGN OPTIONS

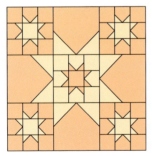

YARDAGE FOR LAP QUILT

45″ × 45″

15″ block

5 blocks plus pieced background blocks

Fabric 1: 1⅞ yards

Fabric 2: 1 yard

CUTTING

Fabric 1:

A (background), B: Cut 2 strips 15½″ × WOF; subcut into 4 squares 15½″ × 15½″ (A-background), and 8 squares 3″ × 3″ (B).

A, C: Cut 5 strips 5½″ × WOF; subcut into 33 squares 5½″ × 5½″ (32A, 1C).

Fabric 2:

A, B (background): Cut 2 strips 8″ × WOF; subcut into 8 squares 8″ × 8″ (B-background), 3 squares 5½″ × 5½″ (A).

A, B, C: Cut 2 strips 5½″ × WOF; subcut into 9 squares 5½″ × 5½″ (5A, 4C) and 10 squares 3″ × 3″ (B).

B: Cut 2 strips 3″ × WOF; subcut into 22 squares 3″ × 3″.

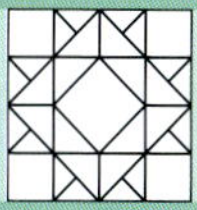

Noon and Light 54

4-GRID

 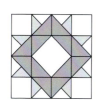 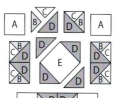 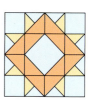

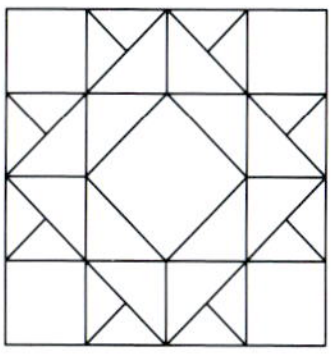

FOR	CUT	NEED	4″	6″	8″	10″	12″
A	4	4	1½	2	2½	3	3½
B	2	8	2¼	2¾	3¼	3¾	4¼
C	2	8	2¼	2¾	3¼	3¾	4¼
D	6	12	1⅞	2⅜	2⅞	3⅜	3⅞
E	1	1	1⅞	2⅝	3⅜	4	4¾

DESIGN OPTIONS

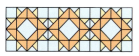

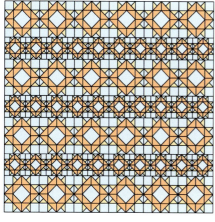

YARDAGE FOR LAP QUILT

60″ × 58″

10″ and 6″ blocks

24 × 10″ + 30 × 6″ = 54 blocks

A, C, E: 2½ yards

B: 1 yard

D: 2 yards

CUTTING

A, 10″: Cut 7 strips 3″ × WOF; subcut into 96 squares 3″ × 3″.

A, 6″: Cut 6 strips 2″ × WOF; subcut into 120 squares 2″ × 2″.

C, 10″: Cut 5 strips 3¾″ × WOF; subcut into 48 squares 3¾″ × 3¾″.

C, 6″: Cut 4 strips 2¾″ × WOF; subcut into 60 squares 2¾″ × 2¾″.

E, 10″: Cut 3 strips 4″ × WOF; subcut into 24 squares 4″ × 4″.

E, 6″: Cut 2 strips 2⅝″ × WOF; subcut into 30 squares 2⅝″ × 2⅝″.

B, 10″: Cut 5 strips 3¾″ × WOF; subcut into 48 squares 3¾″ × 3¾″.

B, 6″: Cut 4 strips 2¾″ × WOF; subcut into 60 squares 2¾″ × 2¾″.

D, 10″: Cut 12 strips 3⅜″ × WOF; subcut into 144 squares 3⅜″ × 3⅜″.

D, 6″: Cut 11 strips 2⅜″ × WOF; subcut into 180 squares 2⅜″ × 2⅜″.

55 North Star

8-GRID

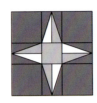
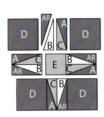

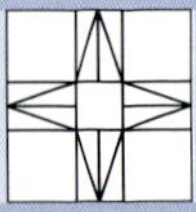

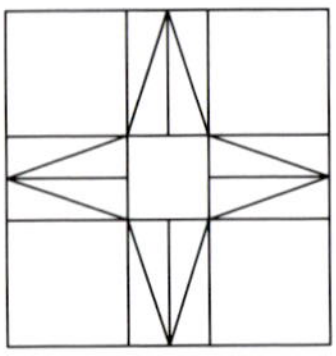

FOR	CUT	NEED	4"	6"	8"	10"	12"
A	2	4	1⅛ × 3⅜	1⅜ × 4⅛	1⅝ × 4⅞	1⅞ × 5⅝	2⅛ × 6⅜
AR	2	4	1⅛ × 3⅜	1⅜ × 4⅛	1⅝ × 4⅞	1⅞ × 5⅝	2⅛ × 6⅜
B	2	4	1⅛ × 3⅜	1⅜ × 4⅛	1⅝ × 4⅞	1⅞ × 5⅝	2⅛ × 6⅜
C	2	4	1⅛ × 3⅜	1⅜ × 4⅛	1⅝ × 4⅞	1⅞ × 5⅝	2⅛ × 6⅜
D	4	4	2	2¾	3½	4¼	5
E	1	1	1½	2	2½	3	3½

DESIGN OPTIONS

YARDAGE FOR WALL HANGING

24" × 28"

4" and 12" blocks

11 × 4" + 1 × 12" = 12 blocks plus background blocks

A, AR, D, Background: 1 yard

B: ¼ yard

C, E: ⅓ yard

CUTTING

A, AR (4", 12"): Cut 1 strip 2⅛" × WOF; subcut into 4 rectangles 2⅛" × 6⅜" (12"), 4 rectangles 1⅛" × 3⅜" (4"). Cut 3 strips 1⅛" × WOF; subcut into 36 rectangles 1⅛" × 3⅜" (4").

A, AR (4"), D (4", 12"): Cut 1 strip 5" × WOF; subcut into 4 squares 5" × 5" (D-12"), 2 squares 2" × 2" (D-4") and 4 rectangles 1⅛" × 3⅜" (2A, 2AR). Cut 2 strips 2" × WOF; subcut into 42 squares 2" × 2" (D-4").

Background: Cut 1 strip 8½" × WOF; subcut into 1 square 8½" × 8½", 4 rectangles 4½" × 8½", and 1 square 4½" × 4½". Cut 1 strip 4½" × WOF; subcut into 9 squares 4½" × 4½".

B (4", 12"): Cut 1 strip 2⅛" × WOF; subcut into 2 rectangles 2⅛" × 6⅜" (12"). Cut 2 strips 1⅛" × WOF; subcut into 22 rectangles 1⅛" × 3⅜" (4").

C (4", 12"): Cut 1 strip 2⅛" × WOF; subcut into 2 rectangles 2⅛" × 6⅜" (12"). Cut 2 strips 1⅛" × WOF; subcut into 22 rectangles 1⅛" × 3⅜" (4").

E (4", 12"): Cut 1 strip 3½" × WOF; subcut into 1 square 3½" × 3½" (12") and 11 squares 1½" × 1½" (4").

Northumberland Star   56

4-GRID

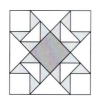
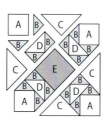

FOR	CUT	NEED	4″	6″	8″	10″	12″
A	4	4	1½	2	2½	3	3½
B	4	16	2¼	2¾	3¼	3¾	4¼
C	1	4	3¼	4¼	5¼	6¼	7¼
D	2	4	1⅞	2⅜	2⅞	3⅜	3⅞
E	1	1	1⅞	2⅝	3⅜	4	4¾

DESIGN OPTIONS

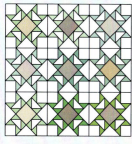

PRECUT FRIENDLY!

Each 12″ block uses:

LC × 1 square for B

LC × ¼ square for E

YARDAGE FOR TWIN QUILT

72″ × 96″

12″ block

6 × 8 setting = 48 blocks

A, C, D: 4⅞ yards

B, E: 60 layer cake squares

CUTTING

NOTE *Mix and match sets of 4B and 1E for each block.*

A: Cut 16 strips 3½″ × WOF; subcut into 192 squares 3½″ × 3½″.

C: Cut 10 strips 7¼″ × WOF; subcut into 48 squares 7¼″ × 7¼″.

D: Cut 10 strips 3⅞″ × WOF; subcut into 96 squares 3⅞″ × 3⅞″.

B: From each of 48 layer cake squares, cut 4 squares 4¼″ × 4¼″.

E: From each of 12 layer cake squares, cut 4 squares 4¾″ × 4¾″.

57 Ohio Star

 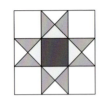 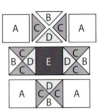

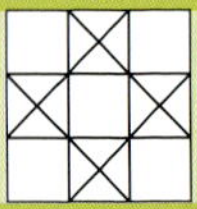

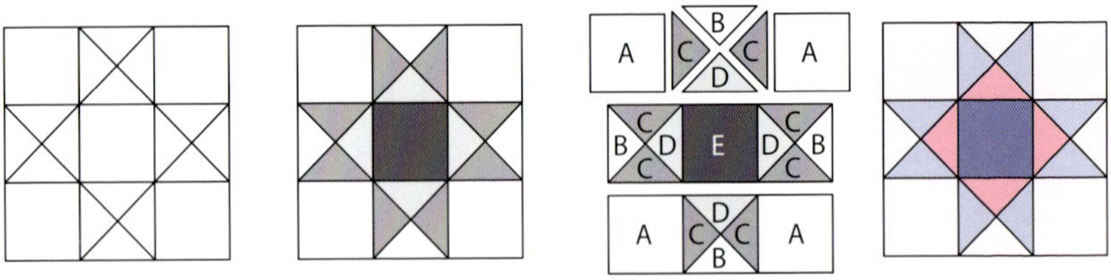

FOR	CUT	NEED	3"	6"	9"	12"	15"
A	4 ☐	4 ☐	1½	2½	3½	4½	5½
B	1 ☐	4 ⊠	2¼	3¼	4¼	5¼	6¼
C	2 ☐	8 ⊠	2¼	3¼	4¼	5¼	6¼
D	1 ☐	4 ⊠	2¼	3¼	4¼	5¼	6¼
E	1 ■	1 ■	1½	2½	3½	4½	5½

DESIGN OPTIONS

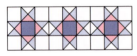

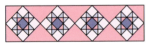

YARDAGE FOR TABLE RUNNER

68″ × 17″

12″ block

4 blocks on diagonal

A, B: ⅝ yard

C: ⅓ yard

D, side and corner triangles: 1 yard

E: ¼ yard

CUTTING

NOTE *Refer to Side and Corner Triangles for Diagonal Settings (page 127).*

A: Cut 2 strips 4½″ × WOF; subcut into 16 squares 4½″ × 4½″.

B: Cut 1 strip 5¼″ × WOF; subcut into 4 squares 5¼″ × 5¼″.

C: Cut 1 strip 5¼″ × WOF; subcut into 8 squares 5¼″ × 5¼″.

D: Cut 1 strip 5¼″ × WOF; subcut into 4 squares 5¼″ × 5¼″.

Side triangles: Cut 1 strip 18¼″ × WOF; subcut into 2 squares 18¼″ × 18¼″.

Corner triangles: Cut 1 strip 9⅜″ × WOF; subcut 2 squares 9⅜″ × 9⅜″.

E: Cut 1 strip 4½″ × WOF; subcut into 4 squares 4½″ × 4½″.

The Original — 58

6-GRID

 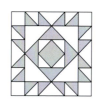  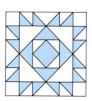

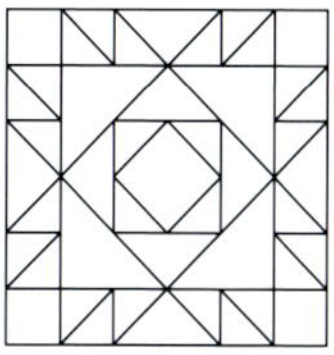

FOR	CUT	NEED	3″	6″	9″	12″	15″
A	4	4	1	1½	2	2½	3
B	8	16	1⅜	1⅞	2⅜	2⅞	3⅜
C	6	12	1⅜	1⅞	2⅜	2⅞	3⅜
D	1	4	2¼	3¼	4¼	5¼	6¼
E	2	4	1⅞	2⅞	3⅞	4⅞	5⅞
F	1	4	2¼	3¼	4¼	5¼	6¼
G	1	1	1¼	1⅞	2⅝	3⅜	4

DESIGN OPTIONS

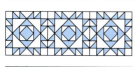
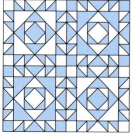

YARDAGE FOR LAP QUILT

60″ × 60″

15″ block

4 × 4 setting = 16 blocks

Fabric 1: 2⅝ yards

Fabric 2: 2⅝ yards

CUTTING

From each fabric:

A: Cut 3 strips 3″ × WOF; subcut into 32 squares 3″ × 3″.

B, C: Cut 10 strips 3⅜″ × WOF; subcut into 112 squares 3⅜″ × 3⅜″ (64B, 48C).

D, F: Cut 3 strips 6¼″ × WOF; subcut into 16 squares 6¼″ × 6¼″ (8D, 8F).

E: Cut 3 strips 5⅞″ × WOF; subcut into 16 squares 5⅞″ × 5⅞″.

G: Cut 1 strip 4″ × WOF; subcut into 8 squares 4″ × 4″.

59 Panama Star

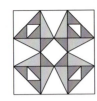
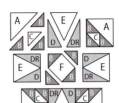
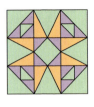

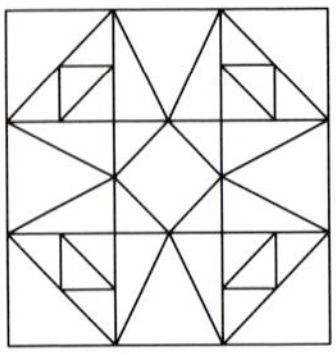

FOR	CUT	NEED	3"	6"	9"	12"	15"
A	2	4	1⅞	2⅞	3⅞	4⅞	5⅞
B	8	16	1⅜	1⅞	2⅜	2⅞	3⅜
C	2	4	1⅜	1⅞	2⅜	2⅞	3⅜
D*	2	4	1½ × 1¾	2¼ × 2½	2¾ × 3½	3¼ × 4½	3¾ × 5½
DR*	2	4	1½ × 1¾	2¼ × 2½	2¾ × 3½	3¼ × 4½	3¾ × 5½
E*	4	4	1½ × 1⅞	2½ × 2⅞	3½ × 3⅞	4½ × 4⅞	5½ × 5⅞
F	1	1	1¼	1⅞	2⅝	3⅜	4

Refer to Triangle in a Square (page 122).

DESIGN OPTIONS

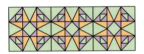

PRECUT FRIENDLY!

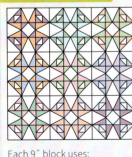

Each 9" block uses:

FQ × ½ fat quarter for B

FQ × ⅓ fat quarter for D, DR

YARDAGE FOR TWIN QUILT

72" × 90"

9" block

8 × 10 setting = 80 blocks

A, C, E, F: 6¼ yards

B, D, DR: 27 fat quarters

CUTTING

NOTE *Mix and match sets of 8B with sets of 2D and 2DR for each block.*

A: Cut 16 strips 3⅞" × WOF; subcut into 160 squares 3⅞" × 3⅞".

C: Cut 10 strips 2⅜" × WOF; subcut into 160 squares 2⅜" × 2⅜".

E: Cut 32 strips 3½" × WOF; subcut into 320 rectangles 3½" × 3⅞".

F: Cut 5 strips 2⅝" × WOF; subcut into 80 squares 2⅝" × 2⅝".

B, D, DR: From each fat quarter, cut 3 strips 2⅜" × WOFQ; subcut into 24 squares 2⅜" × 2⅜" (B). Cut 2 strips 2¾" × WOFQ; subcut 12 rectangles 2¾" × 3½" (D, DR).

8-GRID

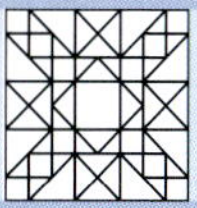

Peacock Star 60

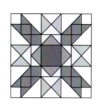

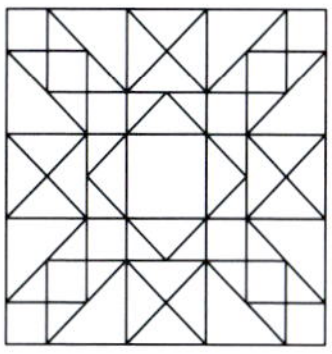

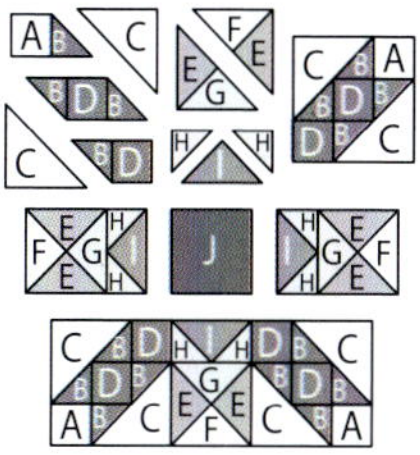

FOR	CUT	NEED	4"	6"	8"	10"	12"
A	4	4	1	1¼	1½	1¾	2
B	8	16	1⅜	1⅝	1⅞	2⅛	2⅜
C	4	8	1⅞	2⅜	2⅞	3⅜	3⅞
D	8	8	1	1¼	1½	1¾	2
E	2	8	2¼	2¾	3¼	3¾	4¼
F	1	4	2¼	2¾	3¼	3¾	4¼
G	1	4	2¼	2¾	3¼	3¾	4¼
H	4	8	1⅜	1⅝	1⅞	2⅛	2⅜
I	1	4	2¼	2¾	3¼	3¾	4¼
J	1	1	1½	2	2½	3	3½

DESIGN OPTIONS

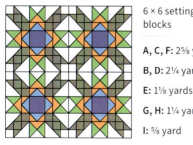

YARDAGE FOR LAP QUILT

72" × 72"

12" block

6 × 6 setting = 36 blocks

A, C, F: 2⅝ yards

B, D: 2¼ yards

E: 1⅛ yards

G, H: 1¼ yards

I: ⅝ yard

J: ½ yard

CUTTING

A: Cut 7 strips 2" × WOF; subcut into 144 squares 2" × 2".

C: Cut 15 strips 3⅞" × WOF; subcut into 144 squares 3⅞" × 3⅞".

F: Cut 4 strips 4¼" × WOF; subcut into 36 squares 4¼" × 4¼".

B: Cut 17 strips 2⅜" × WOF; subcut into 288 squares 2⅜" × 2⅜".

D: Cut 14 strips 2" × WOF; subcut into 288 squares 2" × 2".

E: Cut 8 strips 4¼" × WOF; subcut into 72 squares 4¼" × 4¼".

G: Cut 4 strips 4¼" × WOF; subcut into 36 squares 4¼" × 4¼".

H: Cut 9 strips 2⅜" × WOF; subcut into 144 squares 2⅜" × 2⅜".

I: Cut 4 strips 4¼" × WOF; subcut into 36 squares 4¼" × 4¼".

J: Cut 3 strips 3½" × WOF; subcut into 36 squares 3½" × 3½".

61 Peter Paul Puzzle

 8-GRID

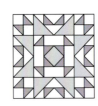
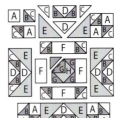

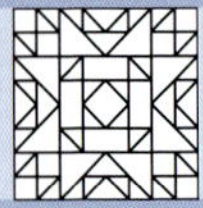

FOR	CUT	NEED	4"	6"	8"	10"	12"
A	8	8	1	1¼	1½	1¾	2
B	10	20	1⅜	1⅝	1⅞	2⅛	2⅜
C	10	20	1⅜	1⅝	1⅞	2⅛	2⅜
D	2	8	2¼	2¾	3¼	3¾	4¼
E	4	8	1⅞	2⅜	2⅞	3⅜	3⅞
F	4	4	1 × 1½	1¼ × 2	1½ × 2½	1¾ × 3	2 × 3½
G*	4	4	1	1¼	1½	1¾	2
H	1	1	1½	2	2½	3	3½

* Refer to Sewing Squares to Squares or Rectangles (page 123).

DESIGN OPTIONS

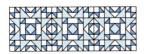

PRECUT FRIENDLY!

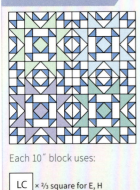

Each 10" block uses:

LC × ⅔ square for E, H

YARDAGE FOR LAP QUILT

60" × 60"

10" block

6 × 6 setting = 36 blocks

A, C, D, F: 3¼ yards

B, G: 1⅝ yards

E, H: 36 layer cake squares

CUTTING

A: Cut 12 strips 1¾" × WOF; subcut into 288 squares 1¾" × 1¾".

C: Cut 19 strips 2⅛" × WOF; subcut into 360 squares 2⅛" × 2⅛".

D: Cut 7 strips 3¾" × WOF; subcut into 72 squares 3¾" × 3¾".

F: Cut 11 strips 1¾" × WOF; subcut into 144 rectangles 1¾" × 3".

B: Cut 19 strips 2⅛" × WOF; subcut into 360 squares 2⅛" × 2⅛".

G: Cut 6 strips 1¾" × WOF; subcut into 144 squares 1¾" × 1¾".

E, H: From each layer cake square, cut 4 squares 3⅜" × 3⅜" (E) and 1 square 3" × 3" (H).

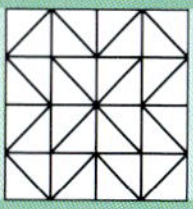

Pieced Star 62

4-GRID

  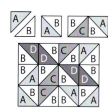 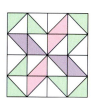

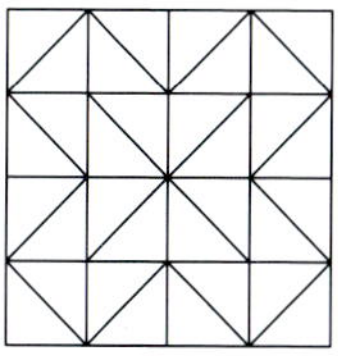

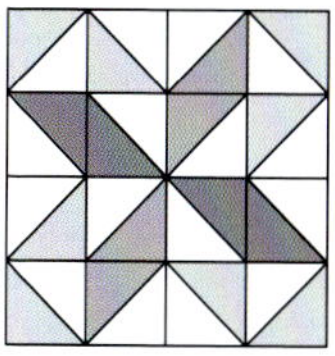

FOR	CUT	NEED	4″	6″	8″	10″	12″
A	4	8	1⅞	2⅜	2⅞	3⅜	3⅞
B	8	16	1⅞	2⅜	2⅞	3⅜	3⅞
C	2	4	1⅞	2⅜	2⅞	3⅜	3⅞
D	2	4	1⅞	2⅜	2⅞	3⅜	3⅞

DESIGN OPTIONS

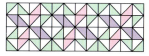

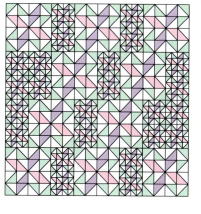

YARDAGE FOR BABY QUILT

48″ × 48″

6″ and 12″ blocks

24 × 6″ and 10 × 12″ = 34 blocks

A: 1 yard
B: 1⅞ yards
C: ⅝ yard
D: ⅝ yard

CUTTING

A, 12″: Cut 4 strips 3⅞″ × WOF; subcut into 40 squares 3⅞″ × 3⅞″.

A, 6″: Cut 6 strips 2⅜″ × WOF; subcut into 96 squares 2⅜″ × 2⅜″.

B, 12″: Cut 8 strips 3⅞″ × WOF; subcut into 80 squares 3⅞″ × 3⅞″.

B, 6″: Cut 12 strips 2⅜″ × WOF; subcut into 192 squares 2⅜″ × 2⅜″.

C, 12″: Cut 2 strips 3⅞″ × WOF; subcut into 20 squares 3⅞″ × 3⅞″.

C, 6″: Cut 3 strips 2⅜″ × WOF; subcut into 48 squares 2⅜″ × 2⅜″.

D, 12″: Cut 2 strips 3⅞″ × WOF; subcut into 20 squares 3⅞″ × 3⅞″.

D, 6″: Cut 3 strips 2⅜″ × WOF; subcut into 48 squares 2⅜″ × 2⅜″.

63 Pineapple Star

3-GRID

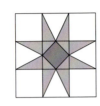

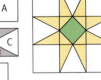

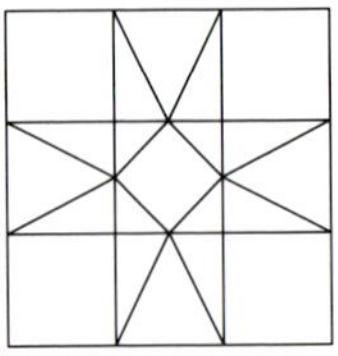

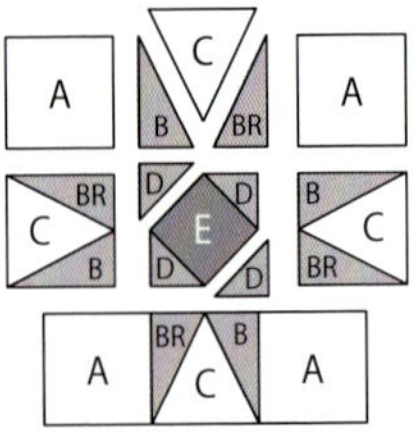

FOR	CUT	NEED	3″	6″	9″	12″	15″
A	4	4	1½	2½	3½	4½	5½
B*	2	4	1½ × 1¾	2¼ × 2½	2¾ × 3½	3¼ × 4½	3¾ × 5½
BR*	2	4	1½ × 1¾	2¼ × 2½	2¾ × 3½	3¼ × 4½	3¾ × 5½
C*	4	4	1½ × 1⅞	2½ × 2⅞	3½ × 3⅞	4½ × 4⅞	5½ × 5⅞
D	2	4	1⅜	1⅞	2⅜	2⅞	3⅜
E	1	1	1¼	1⅞	2⅝	3⅜	4

* *Refer to Triangle in a Square (page 122).*

DESIGN OPTIONS

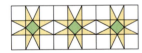

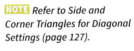

YARDAGE FOR LAP QUILT

63¾″ × 63¾″

15″ block

3 × 3 diagonal setting = 9 blocks plus alternate blocks

A, C: 2 yards

B, BR, D: 1 yard

E, alternate blocks, side and corner triangles: 2⅜ yards

CUTTING

NOTE *Refer to Side and Corner Triangles for Diagonal Settings (page 127).*

A: Cut 6 strips 5½″ × WOF; subcut into 36 squares 5½″ × 5½″.

C: Cut 6 strips 5½″ × WOF; subcut into 36 rectangles 5½″ × 5⅞″.

B, BR: Cut 6 strips 3¾″ × WOF; subcut into 36 rectangles 3¾″ × 5½″.

D: Cut 2 strips 3⅜″ × WOF; subcut into 18 squares 3⅜″ × 3⅜″.

Side and corner triangles: Cut 1 strip 23″ × WOF; subcut into 1 square 22½″ × 22½″ (side triangles), 2 squares 11½″ × 11½″ (corner triangles).

Alternate blocks, side triangles: Cut 1 strip 22½″ × WOF; subcut into 1 square 22½″ × 22½″ (side triangles), 1 square 15½″ × 15½″ (alternate blocks).

Alternate blocks, E: Cut 2 strips 15½″ × WOF; subcut into 3 squares 15½″ × 15½″ (alternate blocks), and 9 squares 4″ × 4″ (E).

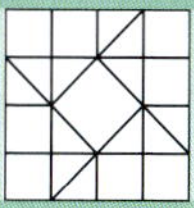

Pinwheel Askew 64

4-GRID

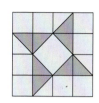
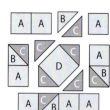
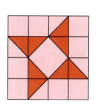

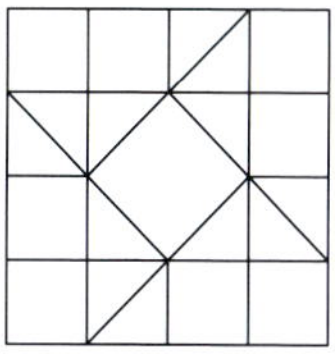

FOR	CUT	NEED	4″	6″	8″	10″	12″
A	8	8	1½	2	2½	3	3½
B	2	4	1⅞	2⅜	2⅞	3⅜	3⅞
C	4	8	1⅞	2⅜	2⅞	3⅜	3⅞
D	1	1	1⅞	2⅝	3⅜	4	4¾

DESIGN OPTIONS

YARDAGE FOR WALL HANGING

32″ × 32″

8″ block

8 blocks plus 5 pieced background blocks

A, B, D, background B, center D: ⅞ yard

C, background C: ½ yard

CUTTING

A: Cut 4 strips 2½″ × WOF; subcut into 64 squares 2½″ × 2½″.

B: Cut 1 strip 2⅞″ × WOF; subcut into 14 squares 2⅞″ × 2⅞″.

B, D: Cut 1 strip 3⅜″ × WOF; subcut into 8 squares 3⅜″ × 3⅜″ (D) and 2 squares 2⅞″ × 2⅞″ (B).

Background B, center D: Cut 1 strip 11⅞″ × WOF; subcut into 1 square 11⅞″ × 11⅞″ (center D) and 2 squares 8⅞″ × 8⅞″, cut in half diagonally (background B).

C: Cut 2 strips 2⅞″ × WOF; subcut into 28 squares 2⅞″ × 2⅞″.

C, background C: Cut 1 strip 8⅞″ × WOF; subcut into 4 squares 8⅞″ × 8⅞″, cut in half diagonally (background C), and 4 squares 2⅞″ × 2⅞″ (C).

65 Prairie Sunrise

10-GRID

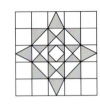
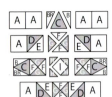
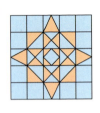

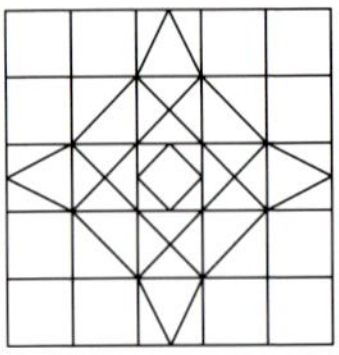

FOR	CUT	NEED	5"	7½"	10"	12½"	15"
A	12	12	1½	2	2½	3	3½
B*	2	4	1½ × 1¾	2 × 2	2¼ × 2½	2½ × 3	2¾ × 3½
BR*	2	4	1½ × 1¾	2 × 2	2¼ × 2½	2½ × 3	2¾ × 3½
C*	4	4	1½ × 1⅞	2 × 2⅜	2½ × 2⅞	3 × 3⅜	3½ × 3⅞
D	2	4	1⅞	2⅜	2⅞	3⅜	3⅞
E	2	4	1⅞	2⅜	2⅞	3⅜	3⅞
F	2	8	2¼	2¾	3¼	3¾	4¼
G	2	8	2¼	2¾	3¼	3¾	4¼
H	2	4	1⅜	1⅝	1⅞	2⅛	2⅜
I	1	1	1¼	1½	1⅞	2¼	2⅝

Refer to Triangle in a Square (page 122).

DESIGN OPTIONS

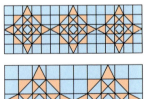
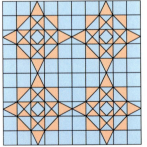

YARDAGE FOR LAP QUILT

60" × 60"
15" block

4 × 4 setting = 16 blocks

A, B, BR, E, F, I: 3¼ yards

C, D, G, H: 2 yards

CUTTING

A: Cut 16 strips 3½" × WOF; subcut into 192 squares 3½" × 3½".

B, BR: Cut 6 strips 2¾" × WOF; subcut into 64 rectangles 2¾" × 3½".

E: Cut 4 strips 3⅞" × WOF; subcut into 32 squares 3⅞" × 3⅞".

F: Cut 4 strips 4¼" × WOF; subcut into 32 squares 4¼" × 4¼".

I: Cut 1 strip 2⅝" × WOF; subcut into 16 squares 2⅝" × 2⅝".

C: Cut 7 strips 3½" × WOF; subcut into 64 rectangles 3½" × 3⅞".

D: Cut 4 strips 3⅞" × WOF; subcut into 32 squares 3⅞" × 3⅞".

G: Cut 4 strips 4¼" × WOF; subcut into 32 squares 4¼" × 4¼".

H: Cut 2 strips 2⅜" × WOF; subcut into 32 squares 2⅜" × 2⅜".

Premium Star — 66

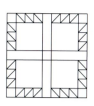 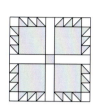 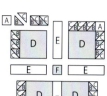 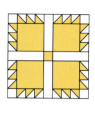

FOR	CUT	NEED	4½″	9″	13½″	18″	22½″
A	4	4	1	1½	2	2½	3
B	12	24	1⅜	1⅞	2⅜	2⅞	3⅜
C	12	24	1⅜	1⅞	2⅜	2⅞	3⅜
D	4	4	2	3½	5	6½	8
E	4	4	1 × 2½	1½ × 4½	2 × 6½	2½ × 8½	3 × 10½
F	1	1	1	1½	2	2½	3

DESIGN OPTIONS

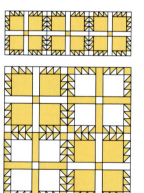

YARDAGE FOR BABY QUILT

54″ × 54″

13½″ block

4 × 4 setting = 16 blocks

Fabric 1: 2 yards

Fabric 2: 2 yards

CUTTING

From each fabric:

A, E, F: Cut 8 strips 2″ × WOF; subcut into 32 rectangles 2″ × 6½″ (E) and 40 squares 2″ × 2″ (32A, 8F).

B, C: Cut 12 strips 2⅜″ × WOF; subcut into 192 squares 2⅜″ × 2⅜″ (96B, 96C).

D: Cut 4 strips 5″ × WOF; subcut into 32 squares 5″ × 5″.

110 Blocks   77

67 President's Star

 3-GRID

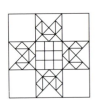
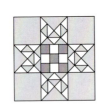
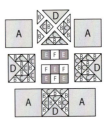
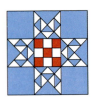

FOR	CUT	NEED	4½″	9″	13½″	18″	22½″
A	4	4	2	3½	5	6½	8
B	7	28	2	2¾	3½	4¼	5
C	5	20	2	2¾	3½	4¼	5
D	1	4	2¾	4¼	5¾	7¼	8¾
E	5	5	1	1½	2	2½	3
F	4	4	1	1½	2	2½	3

DESIGN OPTIONS

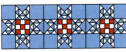
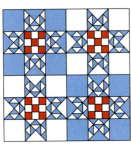

YARDAGE FOR WALL HANGING

36″ × 36″

18″ block

2 × 2 setting = 4 blocks

Fabric 1: 1 yard

Fabric 2: 1 yard

E: ¼ yard

CUTTING

From each of Fabrics 1 and 2:

A: Cut 1 strip 6½″ × WOF; subcut into 6 squares 6½″ × 6½″.

B, C: Cut 3 strips 4¼″ × WOF; subcut into 24 squares 4¼″ × 4¼″ (14B, 10C).

A, D: Cut 1 strip 7¼″ × WOF; subcut into 2 squares 7¼″ × 7¼″ (D) and 2 squares 6½″ × 6½″ (A).

From either Fabric 1 or 2:

F: Cut 1 strip 2½″ × WOF; subcut into 16 squares 2½″ × 2½″.

E: Cut 2 strips 2½″ × WOF; subcut into 20 squares 2½″ × 2½″.

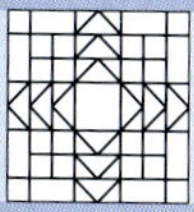

8-GRID

Priscilla's Dream

68

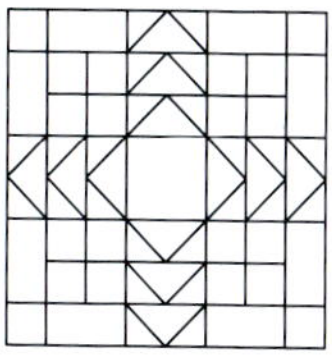
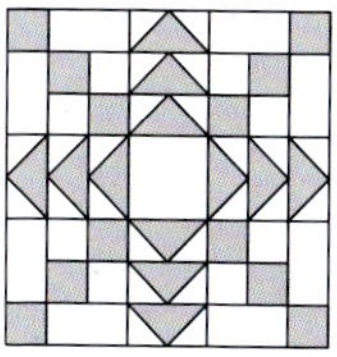
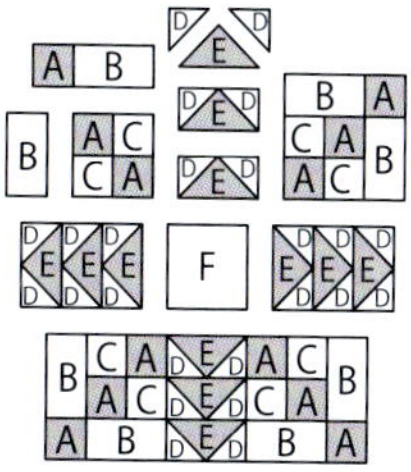
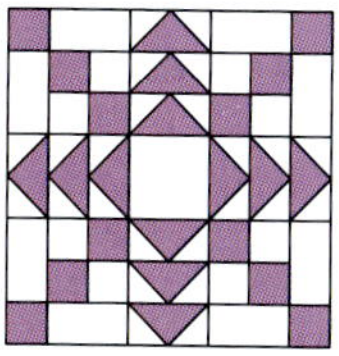

FOR	CUT	NEED	4″	6″	8″	10″	12″
A	12	12	1	1¼	1½	1¾	2
B	8	8	1 × 1½	1¼ × 2	1½ × 2½	1¾ × 3	2 × 3½
C	8	8	1	1¼	1½	1¾	2
D	12	24	1⅜	1⅝	1⅞	2⅛	2⅜
E	3	12	2¼	2¾	3¼	3¾	4¼
F	1	1	1½	2	2½	3	3½

DESIGN OPTIONS

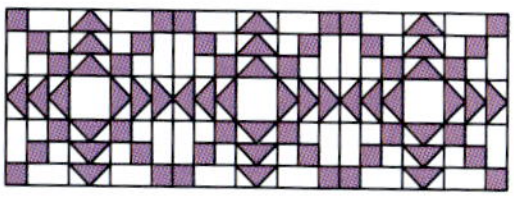

PRECUT FRIENDLY!

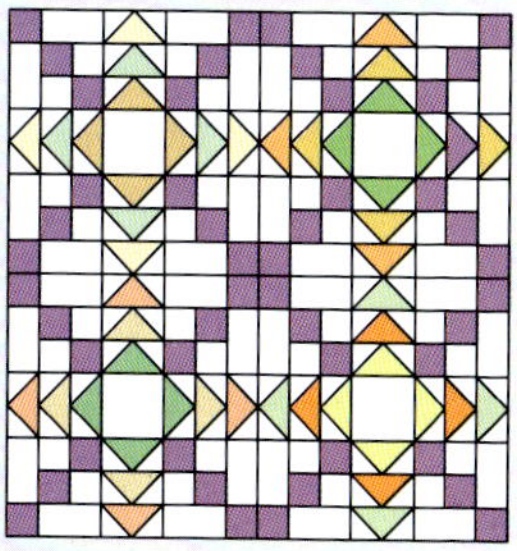

Each 12″ block uses:

CS × 3 squares for E

YARDAGE FOR LAP QUILT

72″ × 72″

12″ block

6 × 6 setting = 36 blocks

A: 1⅜ yards

B, C, D, F: 4⅜ yards

E: 108 charm squares

CUTTING

A: Cut 21 strips 2″ × WOF; subcut into 432 squares 2″ × 2″.

B: Cut 24 strips 2″ × WOF; subcut into 288 rectangles 2″ × 3½″.

C: Cut 14 strips 2″ × WOF; subcut into 288 squares 2″ × 2″.

D: Cut 26 strips 2⅜″ × WOF; subcut into 432 squares 2⅜″ × 2⅜″.

F: Cut 3 strips 3½″ × WOF; subcut into 36 squares 3½″ × 3½″.

E: Trim each charm square to 4¼″ × 4¼″.

69 Providence

 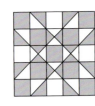 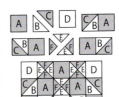 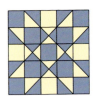

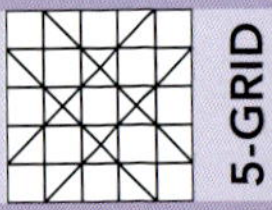

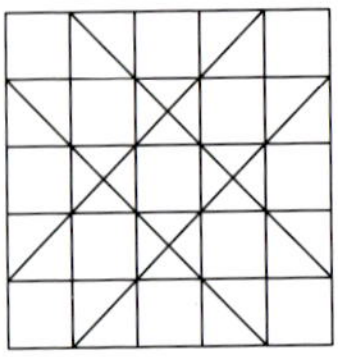

FOR	CUT	NEED	5"	7½"	10"	12½"	15"
A	9	9	1½	2	2½	3	3½
B	4	8	1⅞	2⅜	2⅞	3⅜	3⅞
C	4	8	1⅞	2⅜	2⅞	3⅜	3⅞
D	4	4	1½	2	2½	3	3½
E	2	8	2¼	2¾	3¼	3¾	4¼
F	2	8	2¼	2¾	3¼	3¾	4¼

DESIGN OPTIONS

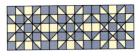

PRECUT FRIENDLY!

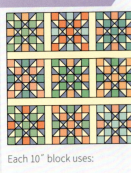

Each 10" block uses:

Jelly roll × ⅔ strip for A
Jelly roll × ¼ strip for D

YARDAGE FOR LAP QUILT

70" × 70"

10" block

6 × 6 setting = 36 blocks

A, D: 36 jelly roll strips

B, E, sashing: 2⅔ yards

C, F: 1⅝ yards

CUTTING

NOTE *Mix and match sets of 9A and 4D for each block.*

A, D: Cut each jelly roll strip into 13 squares 2½" × 2½" (9A, 4D).

B: Cut 11 strips 2⅞" × WOF; subcut into 144 squares 2⅞" × 2⅞".

E: Cut 6 strips 3¼" × WOF; subcut into 72 squares 3¼" × 3¼".

Sashing: Cut 16 strips 2½" × WOF; subcut into 30 rectangles 2½" × 10½". Sew leftover strip and 8 remaining strips together; subcut into 5 strips 2½" × 70½".

C: Cut 11 strips 2⅞" × WOF; subcut into 144 squares 2⅞" × 2⅞".

F: Cut 6 strips 3¼" × WOF; subcut into 72 squares 3¼" × 3¼".

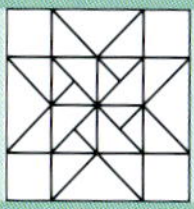

Queen Victoria 70

 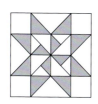 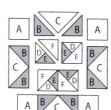 

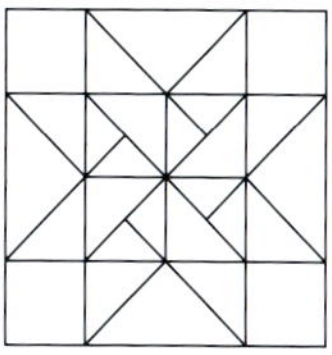

FOR	CUT	NEED	4″	6″	8″	10″	12″
A	4 ☐	4 ☐	1½	2	2½	3	3½
B	4 ▨	8 ◺	1⅞	2⅜	2⅞	3⅜	3⅞
C	1 ☐	4 ⊠	3¼	4¼	5¼	6¼	7¼
D	1 ☐	4 ⊠	2¼	2¾	3¼	3¾	4¼
E	1 ▨	4 ⊠	2¼	2¾	3¼	3¾	4¼
F	2 ☐	4 ◺	1⅞	2⅜	2⅞	3⅜	3⅞

DESIGN OPTIONS

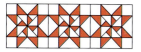

YARDAGE FOR LAP QUILT

72″ × 72″

12″ block

6 × 6 setting = 36 blocks

Fabric 1: 3⅜ yards

Fabric 2: 3⅜ yards

CUTTING

From each fabric:

A: Cut 6 strips 3½″ × WOF; subcut into 72 squares 3½″ × 3½″.

B, F: Cut 11 strips 3⅞″ × WOF; subcut into 108 squares 3⅞″ × 3⅞″ (72B, 36F).

C: Cut 4 strips 7¼″ × WOF; subcut into 18 squares 7¼″ × 7¼″.

D, E: Cut 4 strips 4¼″ × WOF; subcut into 36 squares 4¼″ × 4¼″ (D18, E18).

71 Rainbow Star

6-GRID

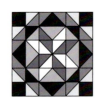
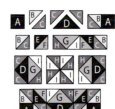
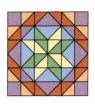

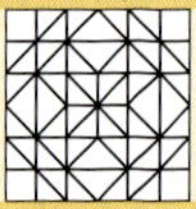

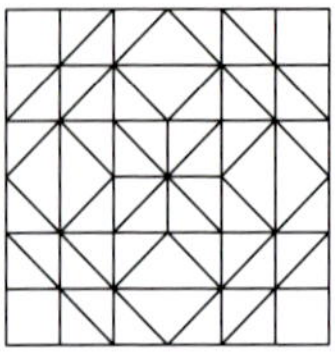

FOR	CUT	NEED	3"	6"	9"	12"	15"
A	4 ■	4 ■	1	1½	2	2½	3
B	4 ☐	8 ◸	1⅜	1⅞	2⅜	2⅞	3⅜
C	8 ▨	16 ◸	1⅜	1⅞	2⅜	2⅞	3⅜
D	1 ■	4 ⊠	2¼	3¼	4¼	5¼	6¼
E	2 ■	4 ◸	1⅜	1⅞	2⅜	2⅞	3⅜
F	2 ▨	4 ◸	1⅜	1⅞	2⅜	2⅞	3⅜
G	1 ▨	4 ⊠	2¼	3¼	4¼	5¼	6¼
H	4 ■	8 ◸	1⅜	1⅞	2⅜	2⅞	3⅜
I	4 ☐	8 ◸	1⅜	1⅞	2⅜	2⅞	3⅜

DESIGN OPTIONS

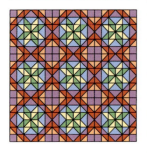

YARDAGE FOR LAP QUILT

72" × 72"

12" block

6 × 6 setting = 36 blocks

A, D, E: 2 yards

B: 1 yard

C: 1⅞ yards

F, G: 1⅜ yards

H: 1 yard

I: 1 yard

CUTTING

A: Cut 9 strips 2½" × WOF; subcut into 144 squares 2½" × 2½".

D, E: Cut 5 strips 5¼" × WOF; subcut into 36 squares 5¼" × 5¼" (D) and 2 squares 2⅞" × 2⅞" (E).

E: Cut 5 strips 2⅞" × WOF; subcut into 70 squares 2⅞" × 2⅞".

B: Cut 11 strips 2⅞" × WOF; subcut into 144 squares 2⅞" × 2⅞".

C: Cut 21 strips 2⅞" × WOF; subcut into 288 squares 2⅞" × 2⅞".

F: Cut 5 strips 2⅞" × WOF; subcut into 70 squares 2⅞" × 2⅞".

F, G: Cut 5 strips 5¼" × WOF; subcut into 36 squares 5¼" × 5¼" (G) and 2 squares 2⅞" × 2⅞" (F).

H: Cut 11 strips 2⅞" × WOF; subcut into 144 squares 2⅞" × 2⅞".

I: Cut 11 strips 2⅞" × WOF; subcut into 144 squares 2⅞" × 2⅞".

Rebel Patch 72

 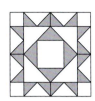 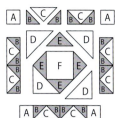 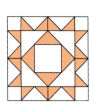

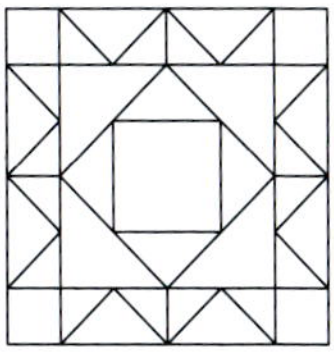

FOR	CUT	NEED	3″	6″	9″	12″	15″
A	4	4	1	1½	2	2½	3
B	8	16	1⅜	1⅞	2⅜	2⅞	3⅜
C	2	8	2¼	3¼	4¼	5¼	6¼
D	2	4	1⅞	2⅞	3⅞	4⅞	5⅞
E	2	4	1⅝	2¼	3	3¾	4⅜
F	1	1	1½	2½	3½	4½	5½

DESIGN OPTIONS

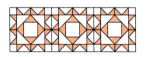

PRECUT FRIENDLY!

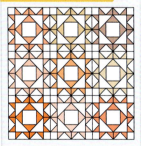

Each 9″ block uses:

LC × ⅔ square for B, E

YARDAGE FOR LAP QUILT

72″ × 72″

9″ block

8 × 8 setting = 64 blocks

A, C, D, F: 4⅝ yards

B, E: 64 layer cake squares

CUTTING

A: Cut 13 strips 2″ × WOF; subcut into 256 squares 2″ × 2″.

C: Cut 15 strips 4¼″ × WOF; subcut into 128 squares 4¼″ × 4¼″.

D: Cut 13 strips at 3⅞″ × WOF; subcut into 128 squares at 3⅞″ × 3⅞″.

F: Cut 6 strips 3½″ × WOF; subcut into 64 squares 3½″ × 3½″.

B, E: From each layer cake square, cut 8 squares 2⅜″ × 2⅜″ (B) and 1 square 4¼″ × 4¼″ (E).

110 Blocks

73 Rhapsody Star

 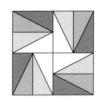 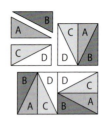 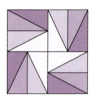

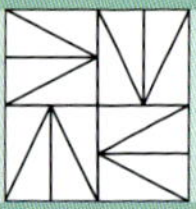

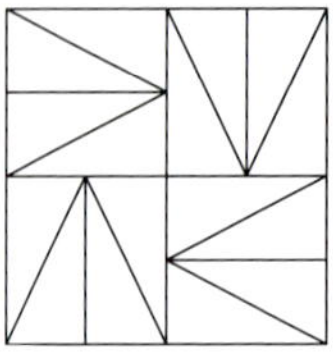

FOR	CUT	NEED	4″	6″	8″	10″	12″
A	2	4	1¾ × 3¼	2¼ × 4¼	2¾ × 5¼	3¼ × 6¼	3¾ × 7¼
B	2	4	1¾ × 3¼	2¼ × 4¼	2¾ × 5¼	3¼ × 6¼	3¾ × 7¼
C	2	4	1¾ × 3¼	2¼ × 4¼	2¾ × 5¼	3¼ × 6¼	3¾ × 7¼
D	2	4	1¾ × 3¼	2¼ × 4¼	2¾ × 5¼	3¼ × 6¼	3¾ × 7¼

DESIGN OPTIONS

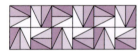

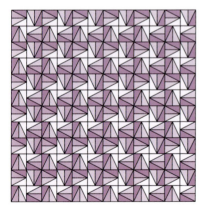

YARDAGE FOR LAP QUILT

72″ × 72″

12″ block

6 × 6 setting = 36 blocks

A, B, C, D: 1⅝ yards each of 4 fabrics

CUTTING

NOTE *Combine 2A, 2B, 2C, and 2D for each block.*

From each fabric:

Cut 7 strips 7¼″ × WOF; subcut into 72 rectangles 3¾″ × 7¼″.

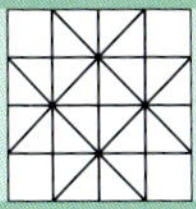

Ribbon Star — 74

 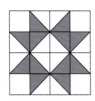 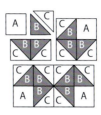 

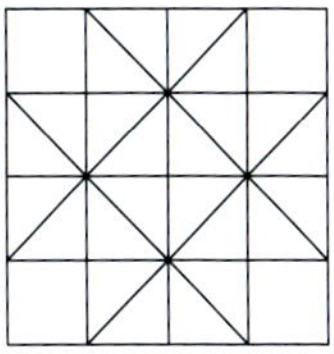

FOR	CUT	NEED	4″	6″	8″	10″	12″
A	4	4	1½	2	2½	3	3½
B	6	12	1⅞	2⅜	2⅞	3⅜	3⅞
C	6	12	1⅞	2⅜	2⅞	3⅜	3⅞

DESIGN OPTIONS

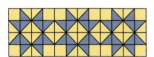

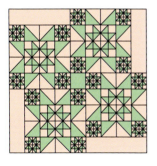

YARDAGE FOR BABY QUILT

54″ × 54″

6″ and 12″ blocks

16 × 6″ + 4 × 12″ = 20 blocks and background blocks

A, C, background: 1⅞ yards

B, background: 2¼ yards

CUTTING

A, 12″: Cut 2 strips 3½″ × WOF; subcut into 16 squares 3½″ × 3½″.

A, 6″: Cut 3 strips 2″ × WOF; subcut into 63 squares 2″ × 2″.

A (6″), C (6″): Cut 6 strips 2⅜″ × WOF; subcut into 96 squares 2⅜″ × 2⅜″ (C) and 1 square 2″ × 2″ (A).

C, 12″: Cut 3 strips 3⅞″ × WOF; subcut into 24 squares 3⅞″ × 3⅞″.

Background HST: Cut 3 strips 6⅞″ × WOF; subcut into 16 squares 6⅞″ × 6⅞″, cut in half diagonally.

B, 12″: Cut 3 strips 3⅞″ × WOF; subcut into 24 squares 3⅞″ × 3⅞″.

B, 6″: Cut 6 strips 2⅜″ × WOF; subcut into 96 squares 2⅜″ × 2⅜″.

Background HST: Cut 3 strips 6⅞″ × WOF; subcut into 16 squares 6⅞″ × 6⅞″, cut in half diagonally.

Background, center square: Cut 4 strips 6½″ × WOF; subcut into 4 rectangles 6½″ × 24½″ and 1 square 6½″ × 6½″ (center).

75 Rising Star

4-GRID

 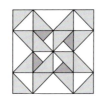 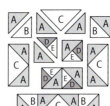 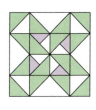

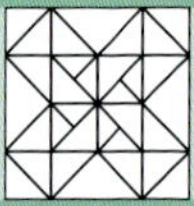

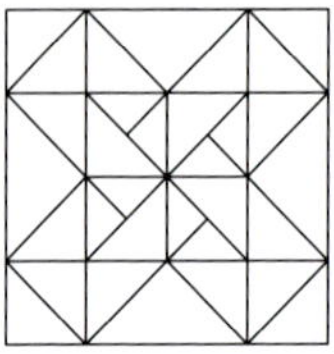

FOR	CUT	NEED	4"	6"	8"	10"	12"
A	8	16	1⅞	2⅜	2⅞	3⅜	3⅞
B	2	4	1⅞	2⅜	2⅞	3⅜	3⅞
C	1	4	3¼	4¼	5¼	6¼	7¼
D	1	4	2¼	2¾	3¼	3¾	4¼
E	1	4	2¼	2¾	3¼	3¾	4¼

DESIGN OPTIONS

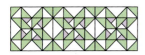

PRECUT FRIENDLY!

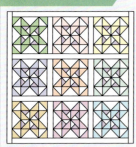

Each 12" block uses:

FQ × ⅓ fat quarter for A

YARDAGE FOR TWIN QUILT

72" × 86"

12" block

5 × 6 setting = 30 blocks

A: 15 fat quarters

B, C, E, Sashing, borders: 4¼ yards

D: ⅝ yard

CUTTING

A: Cut each fat quarter into 16 squares 3⅞" × 3⅞".

B: Cut 6 strips 3⅞" × WOF; subcut into 60 squares 3⅞" × 3⅞".

C: Cut 6 strips 7¼" × WOF; subcut into 30 squares 7¼" × 7¼".

E: Cut 4 strips 4¼" × WOF; subcut into 30 squares 4¼" × 4¼".

Sashing: Cut 8 strips 2½" × WOF; subcut into 24 rectangles 2½" × 12½".

Sashing, borders: Cut 16 strips 2½" × WOF; sew together and subcut into 7 rectangles 2½" × 68½" and 2 rectangles 2½" × 86½".

D: Cut 4 strips 4¼" × WOF; subcut into 30 squares 4¼" × 4¼".

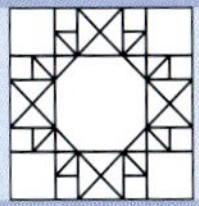

Rising Sun 76

8-GRID

 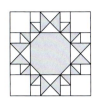 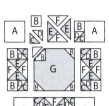 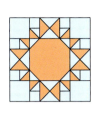

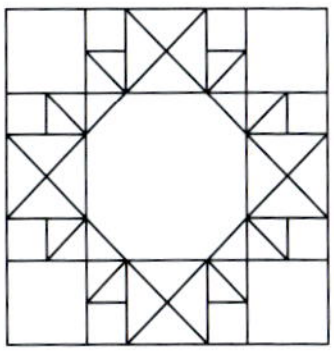

FOR	CUT	NEED	4″	6″	8″	10″	12″
A	4	4	1½	2	2½	3	3½
B*	12	12	1	1¼	1½	1¾	2
C	4	8	1⅜	1⅝	1⅞	2⅛	2⅜
D	4	8	1⅜	1⅝	1⅞	2⅛	2⅜
E	2	8	2¼	2¾	3¼	3¾	4¼
F	2	8	2¼	2¾	3¼	3¾	4¼
G	1	1	2½	3½	4½	5½	6½

Refer to Sewing Squares to Squares or Rectangles (page 123).

DESIGN OPTIONS

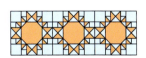

PRECUT FRIENDLY!

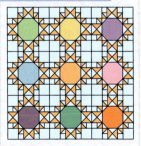

Each 8″ block uses:

CS × 1 square for G

YARDAGE FOR BABY QUILT

48″ × 48″

8″ block

6 × 6 setting = 36 blocks

A, B, D, F: 2½ yards

C, E: 1 yard

G: 36 charm squares

CUTTING

A: Cut 9 strips 2½″ × WOF; subcut into 144 squares 2½″ × 2½″.

B: Cut 16 strips 1½″ × WOF; subcut into 432 squares 1½″ × 1½″.

D: Cut 7 strips 1⅞″ × WOF; subcut into 144 squares 1⅞″ × 1⅞″.

F: Cut 6 strips 3¼″ × WOF; subcut into 72 squares 3¼″ × 3¼″.

C: Cut 7 strips 1⅞″ × WOF; subcut into 144 squares 1⅞″ × 1⅞″.

E: Cut 6 strips 3¼″ × WOF; subcut into 72 squares 3¼″ × 3¼″.

G: Trim each charm square to 4½″ × 4½″.

77 Rocky Mountain Puzzle

 4-GRID

 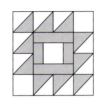 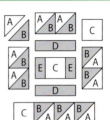 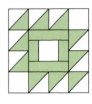

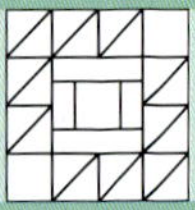

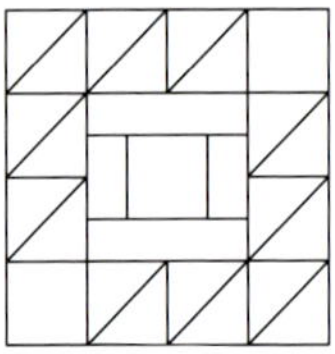

FOR	CUT	NEED	4"	6"	8"	10"	12"
A	5	10	1⅞	2⅜	2⅞	3⅜	3⅞
B	5	10	1⅞	2⅜	2⅞	3⅜	3⅞
C	3	3	1½	2	2½	3	3½
D	2	2	1 × 2½	1¼ × 3½	1½ × 4½	1¾ × 5½	2 × 6½
E	2	2	1 × 1½	1¼ × 2	1½ × 2½	1¾ × 3	2 × 3½

DESIGN OPTIONS

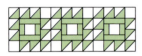

PRECUT FRIENDLY!

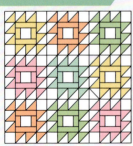

Each 12" block uses:

FQ × ⅔ fat quarter for B, D, E

YARDAGE FOR LAP QUILT

72" × 72"

12" block

6 × 6 setting = 36 blocks

A, C: 3 yards

B, D, E: 18 fat quarters

CUTTING

A: Cut 18 strips 3⅞" × WOF; subcut into 180 squares 3⅞" × 3⅞".

C: Cut 9 strips 3½" × WOF; subcut into 108 squares 3½" × 3½".

B, D, E: From each fat quarter, cut 10 squares 3⅞" × 3⅞" (B), 4 rectangles 2" × 6½" (D), and 4 rectangles 2" × 3½" (E).

Rolling Star 78

 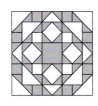 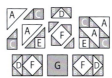 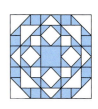

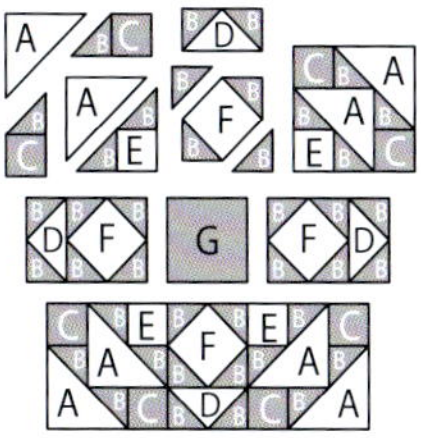

FOR	CUT	NEED	4"	6"	8"	10"	12"
A	4	8	1⅞	2⅜	2⅞	3⅜	3⅞
B	20	40	1⅜	1⅝	1⅞	2⅛	2⅜
C	8	8	1	1¼	1½	1¾	2
D	1	4	2¼	2¾	3¼	3¾	4¼
E	4	4	1	1¼	1½	1¾	2
F	4	4	1¼	1½	1⅞	2¼	2⅝
G	1	1	1½	2	2½	3	3½

DESIGN OPTIONS

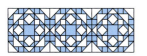

PRECUT FRIENDLY!

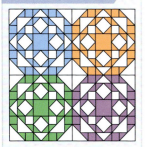

Each 10" block uses:

FQ × ½ fat quarter for B, C, G

YARDAGE FOR QUEEN QUILT

80" × 90"

10" block

8 × 9 setting = 72 blocks

A, D, E, F: 4⅞ yards

B, C, G: 36 fat quarters

CUTTING

A: Cut 24 strips 3⅜" × WOF; subcut into 288 squares 3⅜" × 3⅜".

D: Cut 7 strips 3¾" × WOF; subcut into 72 squares 3¾" × 3¾".

E: Cut 12 strips 1¾" × WOF; subcut into 288 squares 1¾" × 1¾".

F: Cut 16 strips 2¼" × WOF; subcut into 288 squares 2¼" × 2¼".

From each fat quarter:

B: Cut 5 strips 2⅛" × WOFQ; subcut into 40 squares 2⅛" × 2⅛".

C: Cut 2 strips 1¾" × WOFQ; subcut into 16 squares 1¾" × 1¾".

G: Cut 2 squares 3" × 3".

110 Blocks

79 Rose Trellis

 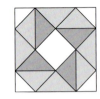 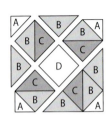 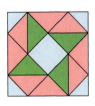

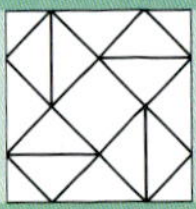

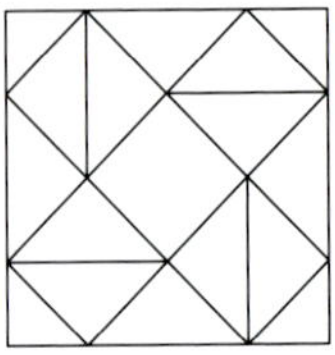

FOR	CUT	NEED	4″	6″	8″	10″	12″
A	2	4	1⅞	2⅜	2⅞	3⅜	3⅞
B	2	8	3¼	4¼	5¼	6¼	7¼
C	1	4	3¼	4¼	5¼	6¼	7¼
D	1	1	1⅞	2⅝	3⅜	4	4¾

DESIGN OPTIONS

PRECUT FRIENDLY!

Each 12″ block uses:

LC × 1 square for B

YARDAGE FOR TABLE RUNNER

12″ × 60″

12″ block

5 blocks

A, D: ⅜ yard

B: 10 layer cake squares

C: ¼ yard

CUTTING

NOTE *Triangle B will be 2 colors in each block.*

A: Cut 1 strip 3⅞″ × WOF; subcut into 10 squares 3⅞″ × 3⅞″.

D: Cut 1 strip 4¾″ × WOF; subcut into 5 squares 4¾″ × 4¾″.

B: Trim each layer cake square to 7¼″ × 7¼″.

C: Cut 1 strip 7¼″ × WOF; subcut into 5 squares 7¼″ × 7¼″.

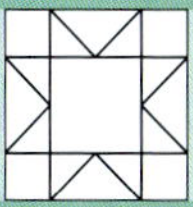

4-GRID

Sawtooth Star 80

 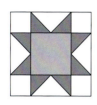 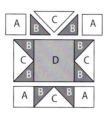 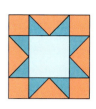

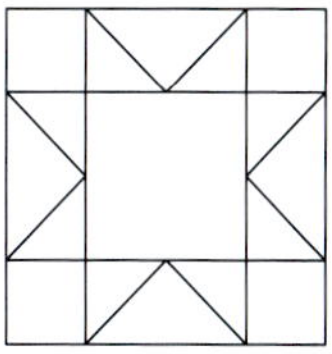

FOR	CUT	NEED	4″	6″	8″	10″	12″
A	4	4	1½	2	2½	3	3½
B	4	8	1⅞	2⅜	2⅞	3⅜	3⅞
C	1	4	3¼	4¼	5¼	6¼	7¼
D	1	1	2½	3½	4½	5½	6½

DESIGN OPTIONS

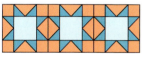

YARDAGE FOR TABLE RUNNER

68″ × 17″

6″ and 12″ blocks

6 × 6″ + 4 × 12″ = 10 blocks

A, C, side triangles: ⅞ yard

B: ½ yard

D: ⅜ yard

CUTTING

NOTE *Refer to Side and Corner Triangles for Diagonal Settings (page 127).*

A, 12″: Cut 1 strip 3½″ × WOF; subcut into 12 squares 3½″ × 3½″.

A (12″, 6″): Cut 1 strip 4″ × WOF; subcut into 4 squares 3½″ × 3½″ (12″) and 24 squares 2″ × 2″ (6″).

C, 12″: Cut 1 strip 7¼″ × WOF; subcut into 4 squares 7¼″ × 7¼″.

Side triangles, C (6″): Cut 1 strip 9¾″ × WOF; subcut into 3 squares 9¾″ × 9¾″ (side triangles) and 6 squares 4¼″ × 4¼″ (C).

B, 12″: Cut 2 strips 3⅞″ × WOF; subcut into 16 squares 3⅞″ × 3⅞″.

B, 6″: Cut 2 strips 2⅜″ × WOF; subcut into 24 squares 2⅜″ × 2⅜″.

D, 12″: Cut 1 strip 6½″ × WOF; subcut into 4 squares 6½″ × 6½″.

D, 6″: Cut 1 strip 3½″ × WOF; subcut into 6 squares 3½″ × 3½″.

81 Seesaw

4-GRID

 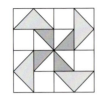 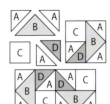 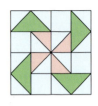

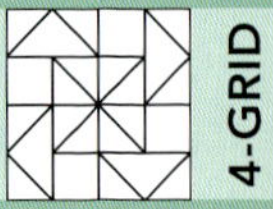

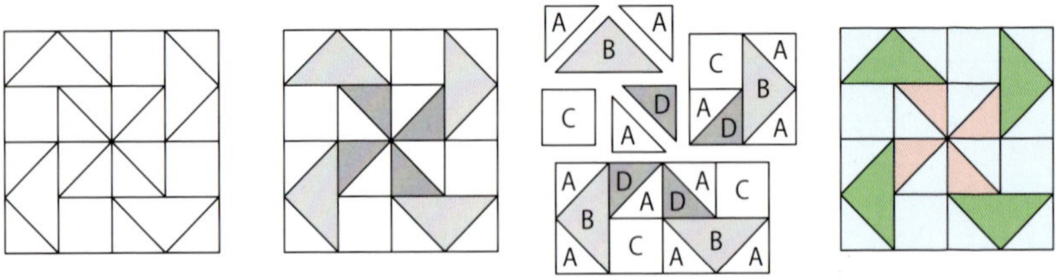

FOR	CUT	NEED	4"	6"	8"	10"	12"
A	6	12	1⅞	2⅜	2⅞	3⅜	3⅞
B	1	4	3¼	4¼	5¼	6¼	7¼
C	4	4	1½	2	2½	3	3½
D	2	4	1⅞	2⅜	2⅞	3⅜	3⅞

DESIGN OPTIONS

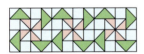

PRECUT FRIENDLY!

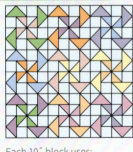

Each 10" block uses:

LC × ½ square for B

LC × ¼ square for D

YARDAGE FOR LAP QUILT

60" × 70"

10" block

6 × 7 setting = 42 blocks

A, C: 3⅛ yards

B, D: 42 layer cake squares

CUTTING

NOTE *Mix and match sets of 1B and 2D for each block.*

A: Cut 21 strips 3⅜" × WOF; subcut into 252 squares 3⅜" × 3⅜".

C: Cut 12 strips 3" × WOF; subcut into 168 squares 3" × 3".

B, D: Cut each layer cake square into 1 square 6¼" × 6¼" (B) and 2 squares 3⅜" × 3⅜" (D).

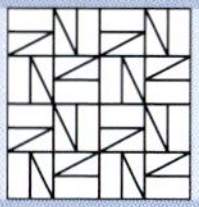

8-GRID

Shooting Stars 82

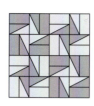
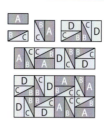

FOR	CUT	NEED	4″	6″	8″	10″	12″
A	8	8	1 × 1½	1¼ × 2	1½ × 2½	1¾ × 3	2 × 3½
B	8	16	1¼ × 2¼	1½ × 2¾	1¾ × 3¼	2 × 3¾	2¼ × 4¼
C	8	16	1¼ × 2¼	1½ × 2¾	1¾ × 3¼	2 × 3¾	2¼ × 4¼
D	8	8	1 × 1½	1¼ × 2	1½ × 2½	1¾ × 3	2 × 3½

DESIGN OPTIONS

PRECUT FRIENDLY!

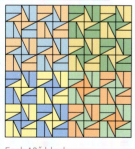

Each 12″ block uses:

FQ × ½ fat quarter for A, B

FQ × ½ fat quarter for C, D

YARDAGE FOR TWIN QUILT

72″ × 96″

12″ block

6 × 8 setting = 48 blocks

A, B, C, D: 48 fat quarters

CUTTING

NOTE *Mix and match sets of AB and CD for each block.*

From each fat quarter:

A, D: Cut 2 strips 3½″ × WOFQ; subcut into 16 rectangles 2″ × 3½″ (8A, 8D).

B, C: Cut 2 strips 4¼″ × WOFQ; subcut into 16 rectangles 2¼″ × 4¼″ (8B, 8C).

110 Blocks 93

83 Silent Star

3-GRID

 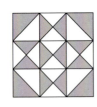 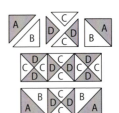 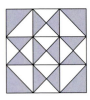

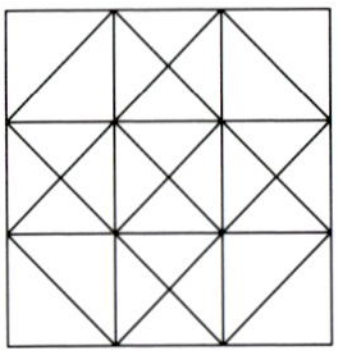

FOR	CUT	NEED	3″	6″	9″	12″	15″
A	2 ▨	4 ◩	1⅞	2⅞	3⅞	4⅞	5⅞
B	2 ☐	4 ◩	1⅞	2⅞	3⅞	4⅞	5⅞
C	3 ☐	10 ⊠	2¼	3¼	4¼	5¼	6¼
D	3 ▨	10 ⊠	2¼	3¼	4¼	5¼	6¼

DESIGN OPTIONS

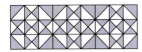
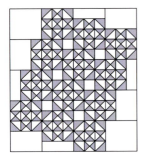

YARDAGE FOR BABY QUILT

48″ × 56″

12″ block

3 × 4 setting = 12 blocks plus background blocks

A, D: 1¼ yards

B, C, background: 2⅛ yards

CUTTING

NOTE *Assemble the quilt in columns. Sew 6 blocks then add columns of the remaining 6 blocks and background blocks as shown.*

A: Cut 3 strips 4⅞″ × WOF; subcut into 24 squares 4⅞″ × 4⅞″.

D: Cut 4 strips 5¼″ × WOF; subcut into 30 squares 5¼″ × 5¼″.

B: Cut 3 strips 4⅞″ × WOF; subcut into 24 squares 4⅞″ × 4⅞″.

C: Cut 4 strips 5¼″ × WOF; subcut into 30 squares 5¼″ × 5¼″.

Background: Cut 2 strips 12½″ × WOF; subcut into 2 squares 12½″ × 12½″, 4 rectangles 12½″ × 8½″, and 4 rectangles 12½″ × 4½″. Cut 1 strip 4½″ × WOF; subcut into 6 squares 4½″ × 4½″.

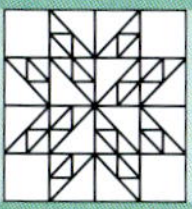

4-GRID

Sparkling Star   84

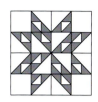
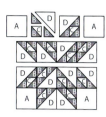
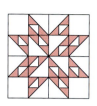

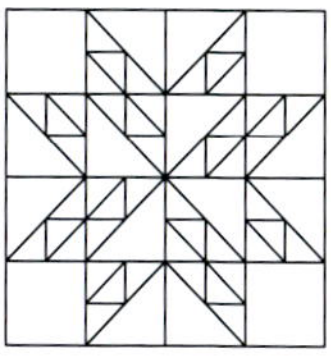

FOR	CUT	NEED	4"	6"	8"	10"	12"
A	4	4	1½	2	2½	3	3½
B	18	36	1⅜	1⅝	1⅞	2⅛	2⅜
C	6	12	1⅜	1⅝	1⅞	2⅛	2⅜
D	6	12	1⅞	2⅜	2⅞	3⅜	3⅞

DESIGN OPTIONS

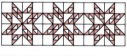

YARDAGE FOR TABLE RUNNER

68" × 17"

12" block

4 blocks

A, C, D: ⅝ yard

B, side and corner triangles: 1 yard

CUTTING

NOTE *Refer to Side and Corner Triangles for Diagonal Settings (page 127).*

A: Cut 1 strip 3½" × WOF; subcut into 12 squares 3½" × 3½".

C: Cut 2 strips 2⅜" × WOF; subcut into 24 squares 2⅜" × 2⅜".

A, D: Cut 3 strips 3⅞" × WOF; subcut into 24 squares 3⅞" × 3⅞" (D), 4 squares 3½" × 3½" (A).

B: Cut 2 strips 2⅜" × WOF; subcut into 31 squares 2⅜" × 2⅜".

B, side triangles: Cut 1 strip 18¼" × WOF; subcut into 2 squares 18¼" × 18¼" (side triangles) and cut 14 squares 2⅜" × 2⅜" (B).

B, corner triangles: Cut 1 strip 9⅜" × WOF; subcut into 2 squares 9⅜" × 9⅜" (corner triangles) and cut 27 squares 2⅜" × 2⅜" (B).

85 Spinning Star

 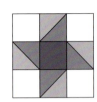 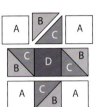 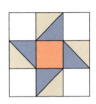

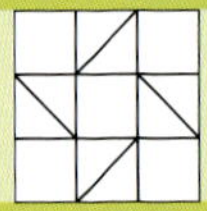

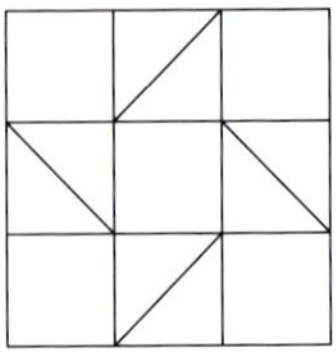

FOR	CUT	NEED	3″	6″	9″	12″	15″
A	4	4	1½	2½	3½	4½	5½
B	2	4	1⅞	2⅞	3⅞	4⅞	5⅞
C	2	4	1⅞	2⅞	3⅞	4⅞	5⅞
D	1	1	1½	2½	3½	4½	5½

DESIGN OPTIONS

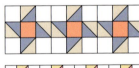

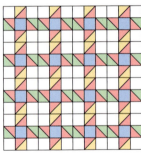

YARDAGE FOR LAP QUILT

60″ × 60″

15″ block

4 × 4 setting = 16 blocks

A: 1¾ yards

B, vertical: ⅔ yard

B, horizontal: ⅔ yard

C: 1 yard

D: ⅝ yard

CUTTING

A: Cut 10 strips 5½″ × WOF; subcut into 64 squares 5½″ × 5½″.

B, vertical: Cut 3 strips 5⅞″ × WOF; subcut into 16 squares 5⅞″ × 5⅞″.

B, horizontal: Cut 3 strips 5⅞″ × WOF; subcut into 16 squares 5⅞″ × 5⅞″.

C: Cut 5 strips 5⅞″ × WOF; subcut into 32 squares 5⅞″ × 5⅞″.

D: Cut 3 strips 5½″ × WOF; subcut into 16 squares 5½″ × 5½″.

Spring Beauty 86

4-GRID

  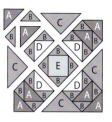 

FOR	CUT	NEED	4″	6″	8″	10″	12″
A	4	8	1⅞	2⅜	2⅞	3⅜	3⅞
B	10	20	1⅝	2	2¼	2⅝	3
C	1	4	3¼	4¼	5¼	6¼	7¼
D	2	4	1⅞	2⅜	2⅞	3⅜	3⅞
E	1	1	1½	2	2½	3	3½

DESIGN OPTIONS

PRECUT FRIENDLY!

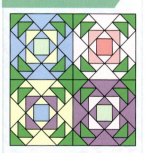

Each 12″ block uses:

FQ × ⅔ fat quarter for B, C

FQ × 1/10 fat quarter for D

FQ × 1/20 fat quarter for E

YARDAGE FOR LAP QUILT

72″ × 72″

12″ block

6 × 6 setting = 36 blocks

A: 1¾ yards

B, C, D, E: 36 fat quarters

CUTTING

NOTE *Mix and match sets of 10B/1C with 2D and 1E for each block.*

A: Cut 15 strips 3⅞″ × WOF; subcut into 144 squares 3⅞″ × 3⅞″.

From each fat quarter:

B: Cut 2 strips 3″ × WOFQ; subcut 10 squares 3″ × 3″.

C, D, E: Cut 1 strip 7¼″ × WOFQ; subcut 1 square 7¼″ × 7¼″ (C), and 2 squares 3⅞″ × 3⅞″ (D) and 1 square 3½″ × 3½″ (E).

110 Blocks

87 Spring Has Come

   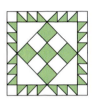

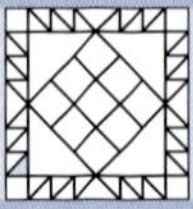

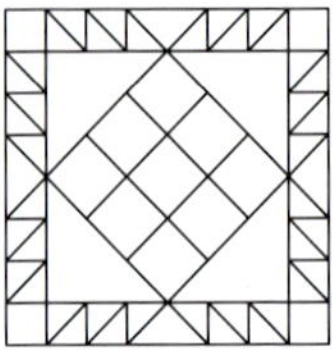

FOR	CUT	NEED	4″	6″	8″	10″	12″
A	4	4	1	1¼	1½	1¾	2
B	12	24	1⅜	1⅝	1⅞	2⅛	2⅜
C	8	16	1⅜	1⅝	1⅞	2⅛	2⅜
D	1	4	2¼	2¾	3¼	3¾	4¼
E	2	4	2⅜	3⅛	3⅞	4⅝	5⅜
F	5	5	1¼	1½	1⅞	2¼	2⅝
G	4	4	1¼	1½	1⅞	2¼	2⅝

DESIGN OPTIONS

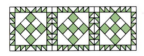

PRECUT FRIENDLY!

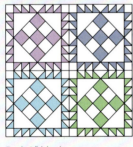

Each 8″ block uses:

LC × ⅔ square for B, F

YARDAGE FOR BABY QUILT

40″ × 40″

8″ block

5 × 5 setting = 25 blocks

A, C, D, E, G: 1⅞ yards

B, F: 25 layer cake squares

CUTTING

A: Cut 4 strips 1½″ × WOF; subcut into 100 squares 1½″ × 1½″.

C, G: Cut 14 strips 1⅞″ × WOF; subcut into 300 squares 1⅞″ × 1⅞″ (200C, 100G).

D: Cut 2 strips 3¼″ × WOF; subcut into 24 squares 3¼″ × 3¼″.

D, E: Cut 5 strips 3⅞″ × WOF; subcut into 50 squares 3⅞″ × 3⅞″ (E) and 1 square 3¼″ × 3¼″ (D).

B, F: From each layer cake square, cut 4 strips 1⅞″ × 10″; subcut 17 squares 1⅞″ × 1⅞″ (12B, 5F).

4-GRID

Square and Star   88

  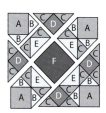 

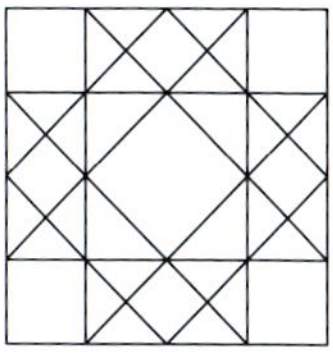

FOR	CUT	NEED	4″	6″	8″	10″	12″
A	4	4	1½	2	2½	3	3½
B	2	8	2¼	2¾	3¼	3¾	4¼
C	4	16	2¼	2¾	3¼	3¾	4¼
D	4	4	1¼	1½	1⅞	2¼	2⅝
E	2	4	1⅞	2⅜	2⅞	3⅜	3⅞
F	1	1	1⅞	2⅝	3⅜	4	4¾

DESIGN OPTIONS

PRECUT FRIENDLY!

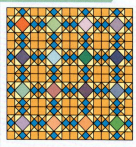

Each 12″ block uses:

CS × 1 square for F

YARDAGE FOR TWIN QUILT

72″ × 96″

12″ block

6 × 8 setting = 48 blocks

A, C: 4⅜ yards

B, E: 2⅝ yards

D: 1 yard

F: 48 charm squares

CUTTING

A: Cut 16 strips 3½″ × WOF; subcut into 192 squares 3½″ × 3½″.

C: Cut 22 strips 4¼″ × WOF; subcut into 192 squares 4¼″ × 4¼″.

B: Cut 11 strips 4¼″ × WOF; subcut into 96 squares 4¼″ × 4¼″.

E: Cut 10 strips 3⅞″ × WOF; subcut into 96 squares 3⅞″ × 3⅞″.

D: Cut 12 strips 2⅝″ × WOF; subcut into 192 squares 2⅝″ × 2⅝″.

F: Trim each charm square to 4¾″ × 4¾″.

89 Square in Square Star

3-GRID

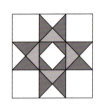
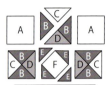
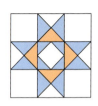

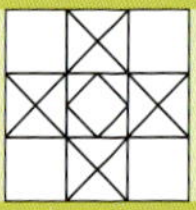

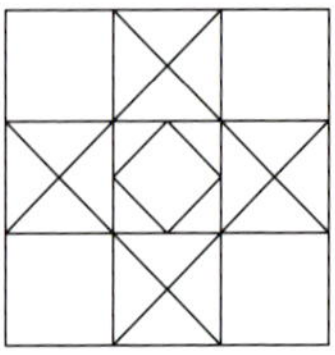

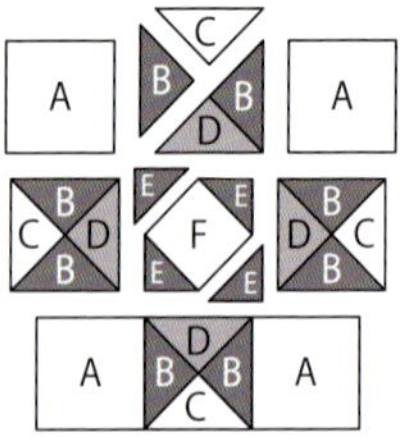

FOR	CUT	NEED	3″	6″	9″	12″	15″
A	4 ☐	4 ☐	1½	2½	3½	4½	5½
B	2 ■	8 ⊠	2¼	3¼	4¼	5¼	6¼
C	1 ☐	4 ⊠	2¼	3¼	4¼	5¼	6¼
D	1 ▨	4 ⊠	2¼	3¼	4¼	5¼	6¼
E	2 ■	4 ◪	1⅜	1⅞	2⅜	2⅞	3⅜
F	1 ☐	1 ☐	1¼	1⅞	2⅝	3⅜	4

DESIGN OPTIONS

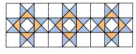
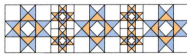

YARDAGE FOR TABLE RUNNER

48″ × 12″

6″ and 12″ blocks

4 × 6″ + 3 × 12″ = 7 blocks

A, C, F: ⅝ yard

Fabric 1: ½ yard

Fabric 2: ½ yard

CUTTING

A (12″), C (12″): Cut 1 strip 5¼″ × WOF; subcut into 3 squares 5¼″ × 5¼″ (C) and 4 squares 4½″ × 4½″ (A).

A, 12″: Cut 1 strip 4½″ × WOF; subcut into 8 squares 4½″ × 4½″.

C (6″), F (6″, 12″): Cut 1 strip 3⅜″ × WOF; subcut into 3 squares 3⅜″ × 3⅜″ (F-12″), 4 squares 3¼″ × 3¼″ (C) and 4 squares 1⅞″ × 1⅞″ (F-6″).

A, 6″: Cut 1 strip 2½″ × WOF; subcut into 16 squares 2½″ × 2½″.

Fabric 1:

B (12″), E (6″): Cut 1 strip 5¼″ × WOF; subcut into 6 squares 5¼″ × 5¼″ (B) and 8 squares 1⅞″ × 1⅞″ (E).

D, 6″: Cut 1 strip 3¼″ × WOF; subcut into 4 squares 3¼″ × 3¼″.

Fabric 2:

D (12″), E (12″): Cut 1 strip 5¼″ × WOF; subcut into 3 squares 5¼″ × 5¼″ (D) and 6 squares 2⅞″ × 2⅞″ (E).

B, 6″: Cut 1 strip 3¼″ × WOF; subcut into 8 squares 3¼″ × 3¼″.

Star Block 90

4-GRID

 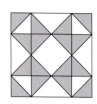 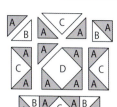 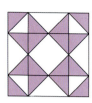

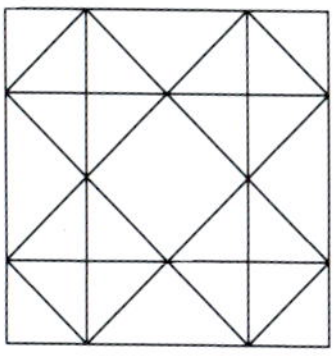

FOR	CUT	NEED	4″	6″	8″	10″	12″
A	8	16	1⅞	2⅜	2⅞	3⅜	3⅞
B	2	4	1⅞	2⅜	2⅞	3⅜	3⅞
C	1	4	3¼	4¼	5¼	6¼	7¼
D	1	1	1⅞	2⅝	3⅜	4	4¾

DESIGN OPTIONS

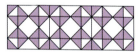

PRECUT FRIENDLY!

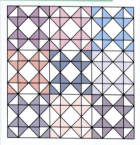

Each 8″ block uses:

LC × 1 square for A

YARDAGE FOR BABY QUILT

48″ × 56″

8″ block

6 × 7 setting = 42 blocks

A: 42 layer cake squares

B, C, D: 1⅞ yards

CUTTING

A: From each layer cake square, cut 8 squares 2⅞″ × 2⅞″.

B: Cut 6 strips 2⅞″ × WOF; subcut into 84 squares 2⅞″ × 2⅞″.

C: Cut 6 strips 5¼″ × WOF; subcut into 42 squares 5¼″ × 5¼″.

D: Cut 4 strips 3⅜″ × WOF; subcut into 42 squares 3⅜″ × 3⅜″.

110 Blocks

91 Stardust

4-GRID

 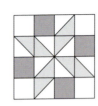 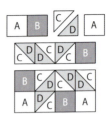 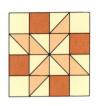

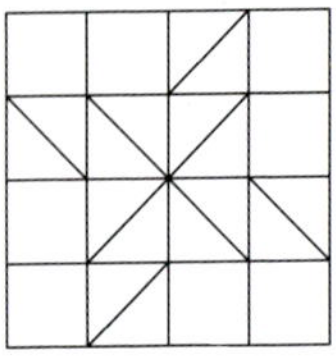

FOR	CUT	NEED	4″	6″	8″	10″	12″
A	4	4	1½	2	2½	3	3½
B	4	4	1½	2	2½	3	3½
C	4	8	1⅞	2⅜	2⅞	3⅜	3⅞
D	4	8	1⅞	2⅜	2⅞	3⅜	3⅞

DESIGN OPTIONS

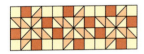

PRECUT FRIENDLY!

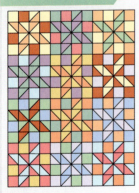

Each 12″ block uses:

- FQ × ¼ fat quarter for A
- FQ × ¼ fat quarter for B
- FQ × ¼ fat quarter for C
- FQ × ¼ fat quarter for D

YARDAGE FOR TWIN QUILT

72″ × 84″

12″ block

6 × 7 setting = 42 blocks

A, B, C, D: 42 fat quarters

CUTTING

NOTE *Mix and match sets of 4A/4C with 4B and 4D for each block.*

From each fat quarter:

A, B: Cut 2 strips 3½″ × WOFQ; subcut into 8 squares 3½″ × 3½″ (4A, 4B).

C, D: Cut 2 strips 3⅞″ × WOFQ; subcut into 8 squares 3⅞″ × 3⅞″ (4C, 4D).

6-GRID

Star Gardner 92

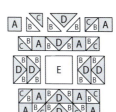
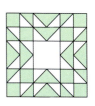

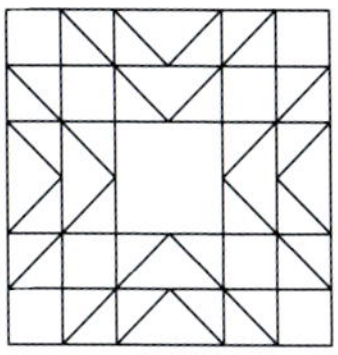

FOR	CUT	NEED	3"	6"	9"	12"	15"
A	8	8	1	1½	2	2½	3
B	12	24	1⅜	1⅞	2⅜	2⅞	3⅜
C	4	8	1⅜	1⅞	2⅜	2⅞	3⅜
D	2	8	2¼	3¼	4¼	5¼	6¼
E	1	1	1½	2½	3½	4½	5½

DESIGN OPTIONS

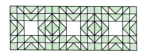

YARDAGE FOR BABY QUILT

36" × 36"

6" block

6 × 6 setting = 36 blocks

A, C, D: 1½ yards

B, E: 1½ yards

CUTTING

A: Cut 11 strips 1½" × WOF; subcut into 288 squares 1½" × 1½".

C: Cut 7 strips 1⅞" × WOF; subcut into 144 squares 1⅞" × 1⅞".

D: Cut 6 strips 3¼" × WOF; subcut into 72 squares 3¼" × 3¼".

B: Cut 20 strips 1⅞" × WOF; subcut into 432 squares 1⅞" × 1⅞".

E: Cut 3 strips 2½" × WOF; subcut into 36 squares 2½" × 2½".

110 Blocks

93 Star of Alamo

6-GRID

 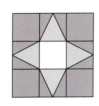 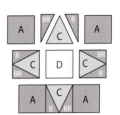

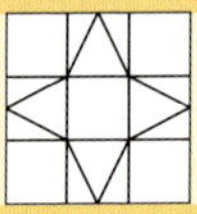

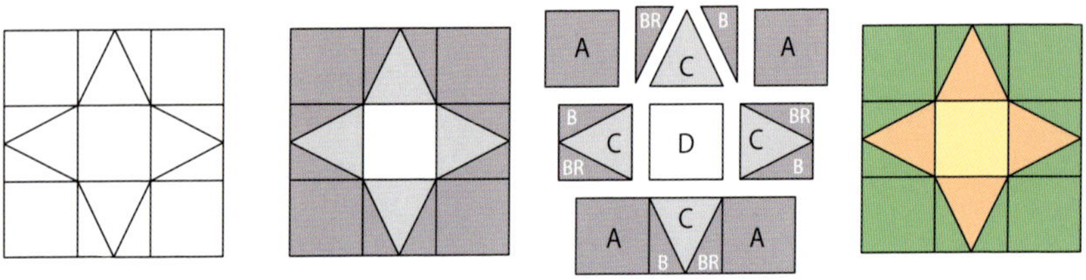

FOR	CUT	NEED	3″	6″	9″	12″	15″
A	4 □	4 □	1½	2½	3½	4½	5½
B*	2 ▭	4 ◨	1½ × 1¾	2¼ × 2½	2¾ × 3½	3¼ × 4½	3¾ × 5½
BR*	2 ▭	4 ◨	1½ × 1¾	2¼ × 2½	2¾ × 3½	3¼ × 4½	3¾ × 5½
C*	4 ▭	4 △	1½ × 1⅞	2½ × 2⅞	3½ × 3⅞	4½ × 4⅞	5½ × 5⅞
D	1 □	1 □	1½	2½	3½	4½	5½

* Refer to Triangle in a Square (page 122).

DESIGN OPTIONS

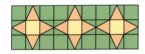

PRECUT FRIENDLY!

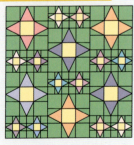

Each 6″ block uses:

LC × ½ square for C

Each 12″ block uses:

LC × 1 for C

YARDAGE FOR BABY QUILT

36″ × 36″

6″ and 12″ blocks

12 × 6″ + 6 × 12″ = 18 blocks

A, B, BR: 1¼ yards

C: 12 layer cake squares

D: ⅓ yard

CUTTING

A, 12″: Cut 3 strips 4½″ × WOF; subcut into 24 squares 4½″ × 4½″.

A, 6″: Cut 3 strips 2½″ × WOF; subcut into 48 squares 2½″ × 2½″.

B, 12″: Cut 3 strips 3¼″ × WOF; subcut into 24 rectangles 3¼″ × 4½″.

B, 6″: Cut 3 strips 2¼″ × WOF; subcut into 48 rectangles 2¼″ × 2½″.

C, 12″: From each of 6 layer cake squares, cut 4 rectangles 4½″ × 4⅞″.

C, 6″: From each of 6 layer cake squares, cut 8 rectangles 2½″ × 2⅞″.

D, 12″: Cut 1 strip 4½″ × WOF; subcut into 6 squares 4½″ × 4½″.

D, 6″: Cut 1 strip 2½″ × WOF; subcut into 12 squares 2½″ × 2½″.

Star of Bethlehem 94

4-GRID

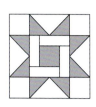
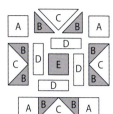

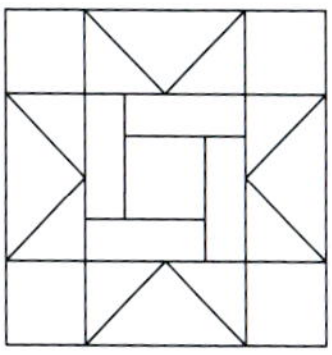

FOR	CUT	NEED	4″	6″	8″	10″	12″
A	4 ☐	4 ☐	1½	2	2½	3	3½
B	4 ▨	8 ◰	1⅞	2⅜	2⅞	3⅜	3⅞
C	1 ☐	4 ⊠	3¼	4¼	5¼	6¼	7¼
D*	4 ▭	4 ▭	1 × 2	1¼ × 2¾	1½ × 3½	1¾ × 4¼	2 × 5
E*	1 ▨	1 ▨	1½	2	2½	3	3½

*Refer to Sewing Partial Seams (page 123).

DESIGN OPTIONS

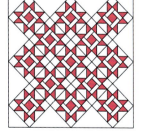

YARDAGE FOR BABY QUILT

34″ × 34″

8″ block

3 × 3 on point setting = 13 blocks

A, C, D, side and corner triangles: 1⅜ yards

B, E: ½ yard

CUTTING

NOTE *Refer to Side and Corner Triangles for Diagonal Settings (page 127).*

A: Cut 4 strips 2½″ × WOF; subcut into 52 squares 2½″ × 2½″.

C: Cut 2 strips 5¼″ × WOF; subcut into 13 squares 5¼″ × 5¼″.

D: Cut 2 strips 3½″ × WOF; subcut into 52 rectangles 1½″ × 3½″.

Side and corner triangles: Cut 1 strip 12⅝″ × WOF; subcut into 2 squares 12⅝″ × 12⅝″ (side triangles), 2 squares 6⅝″ × 6⅝″ (corner triangles).

B: Cut 4 strips 2⅞″ × WOF; subcut into 52 squares 2⅞″ × 2⅞″.

E: Cut 1 strip 2½″ × WOF; subcut into 13 squares 2½″ × 2½″.

95 Star of Hope

 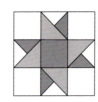 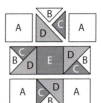 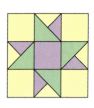

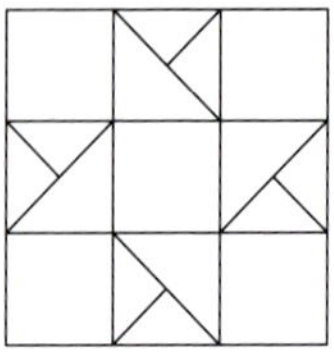

FOR	CUT	NEED	3″	6″	9″	12″	15″
A	4 ☐	4 ☐	1½	2½	3½	4½	5½
B	1 ☐	4 ⊠	2¼	3¼	4¼	5¼	6¼
C	1 ☐	4 ⊠	2¼	3¼	4¼	5¼	6¼
D	2 ☐	4 ◩	1⅞	2⅞	3⅞	4⅞	5⅞
E	1 ☐	1 ☐	1½	2½	3½	4½	5½

DESIGN OPTIONS

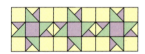

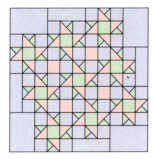

YARDAGE FOR LAP QUILT

55″ × 55″

15″ block

3 × 3 setting = 9 blocks

A, B, background: 2⅜ yards

C, E: ⅞ yard

D, background: ⅞ yard

CUTTING

NOTE *Quilt can be assembled in rows with partial blocks, or in sections with partial seams. Refer to Sewing Partial Seams (page 123).*

A: Cut 6 strips 5½″ × WOF; subcut into 36 squares 5½″ × 5½″.

B: Cut 2 strips 6¼″ × WOF; subcut into 9 squares 6¼″ × 6¼″.

Background: Cut 2 strips 15½″ × WOF; subcut into 4 rectangles 10½″ × 15½″ and 4 rectangles 5½″ × 15½″.

C: Cut 2 strips 6¼″ × WOF; subcut into 9 squares 6¼″ × 6¼″.

E: Cut 2 strips 5½″ × WOF; subcut into 9 squares 5½″ × 5½″.

D: Cut 3 strips 5⅞″ × WOF; subcut into 18 squares 5⅞″ × 5⅞″.

Background: Cut 1 strip 5½″ × WOF; subcut into 4 squares 5½″ × 5½″.

Star of Many Points — 96

4-GRID

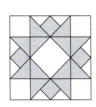
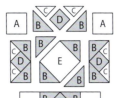
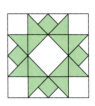

FOR	CUT	NEED	4″	6″	8″	10″	12″
A	4	4	1½	2	2½	3	3½
B	6	12	1⅞	2⅜	2⅞	3⅜	3⅞
C	2	8	2¼	2¾	3¼	3¾	4¼
D	4	4	1¼	1½	1⅞	2¼	2⅝
E	1	1	1⅞	2⅝	3⅜	4	4¾

DESIGN OPTIONS

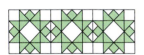

PRECUT FRIENDLY!

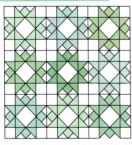

Each 8″ block uses:

LC × ⅔ square for B, D

YARDAGE FOR LAP QUILT

64″ × 64″

8″ block

8 × 8 setting = 64 blocks

A, C, E: 2⅞ yards

B, D: 64 layer cake squares

CUTTING

A: Cut 16 strips 2½″ × WOF; subcut into 256 squares 2½″ × 2½″.

C: Cut 11 strips 3¼″ × WOF; subcut into 128 squares 3¼″ × 3¼″.

E: Cut 6 strips 3⅜″ × WOF; subcut into 64 squares 3⅜″ × 3⅜″.

B, D: From each layer cake square, cut 6 squares 2⅞″ × 2⅞″ (B) and 4 squares 1⅞″ × 1⅞″ (D).

110 Blocks

97 Star of Sedona

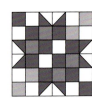

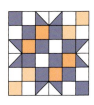

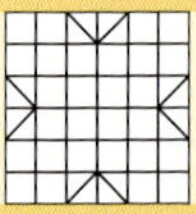

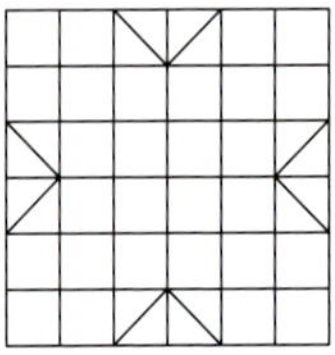

FOR	CUT	NEED	3″	6″	9″	12″	15″
A	10	10	1	1½	2	2½	3
B	10	10	1	1½	2	2½	3
C	4	8	1⅜	1⅞	2⅜	2⅞	3⅜
D	4	8	1⅜	1⅞	2⅜	2⅞	3⅜
E	4	4	1	1½	2	2½	3
F	4	4	1	1½	2	2½	3

DESIGN OPTIONS

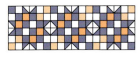
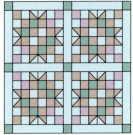

YARDAGE FOR TWIN QUILT

72″ × 84″

12″ block

5 × 6 setting = 30 blocks plus sashing and cornerstones

A, C: 2¼ yards

B, D, sashing: 4 yards

E, cornerstones: ⅞ yard

F: ⅝ yard

CUTTING

A: Cut 19 strips 2½″ × WOF; subcut into 300 squares 2½″ × 2½″.

C: Cut 9 strips 2⅞″ × WOF; subcut into 120 squares 2⅞″ × 2⅞″.

B: Cut 19 strips 2½″ × WOF; subcut into 300 squares 2½″ × 2½″.

D: Cut 9 strips 2⅞″ × WOF; subcut into 120 squares 2⅞″ × 2⅞″.

Sashing: Cut 24 strips 2½″ × WOF; subcut into 71 rectangles 2½″ × 12½″.

E, cornerstones: Cut 11 strips 2½″ × WOF; subcut into 162 squares 2½″ × 2½″ (120E, 42 cornerstones).

F: Cut 8 strips 2½″ × WOF; subcut into 120 squares 2½″ × 2½″.

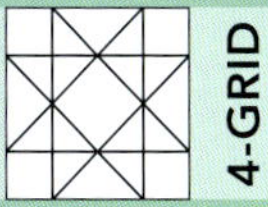

Star of Virginia 98

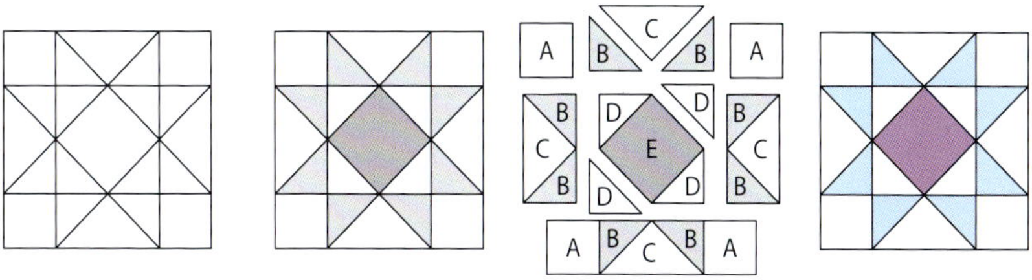

4-GRID

 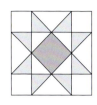 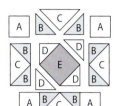 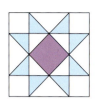

FOR	CUT	NEED	4″	6″	8″	10″	12″
A	4	4	1½	2	2½	3	3½
B	4	8	1⅞	2⅜	2⅞	3⅜	3⅞
C	1	4	3¼	4¼	5¼	6¼	7¼
D	2	4	1⅞	2⅜	2⅞	3⅜	3⅞
E	1	1	1⅞	2⅝	3⅜	4	4¾

DESIGN OPTIONS

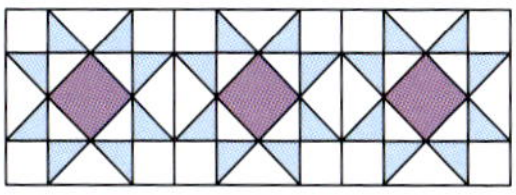

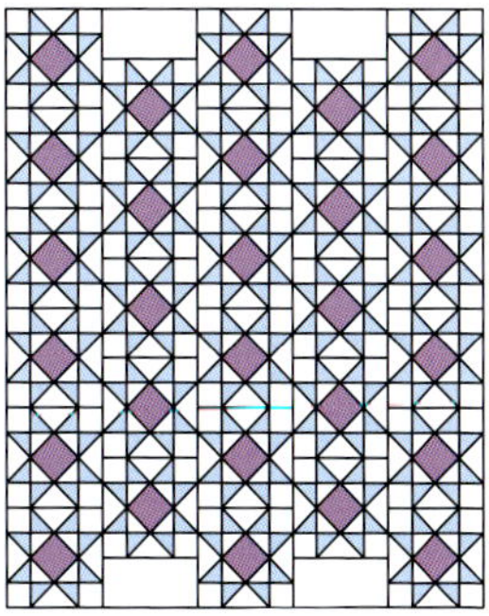

YARDAGE FOR LAP QUILT

50″ × 60″

10″ block

5 × 6 staggered setting = 28 blocks

A, C, D, background: 2⅜ yards

B: 1⅛ yards

E: ½ yard

CUTTING

A: Cut 8 strips 3″ × WOF; subcut into 112 squares 3″ × 3″.

C: Cut 5 strips 6¼″ × WOF; subcut into 28 squares 6¼″ × 6¼″.

D: Cut 5 strips 3⅜″ × WOF; subcut into 56 squares 3⅜″ × 3⅜″.

Background: Cut 1 strip 5½″ × WOF; subcut into 4 rectangles 5½″ × 10½″.

B: Cut 10 strips 3⅜″ × WOF; subcut into 112 squares 3⅜″ × 3⅜″.

E: Cut 3 strips 4″ × WOF; subcut into 28 squares 4″ × 4″.

99 Star Pattern

 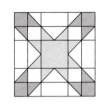  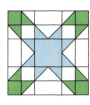

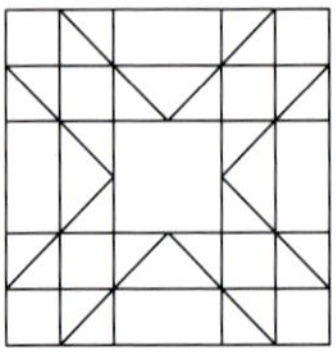

FOR	CUT	NEED	3"	6"	9"	12"	15"
A	4	4	1	1½	2	2½	3
B	4	8	1⅜	1⅞	2⅜	2⅞	3⅜
C	4	8	1⅜	1⅞	2⅜	2⅞	3⅜
D	4	4	1	1½	2	2½	3
E	4	4	1 × 1½	1½ × 2½	2 × 3½	2½ × 4½	3 × 5½
F	1	4	2¼	3¼	4¼	5¼	6¼
G	4	8	1⅜	1⅞	2⅜	2⅞	3⅜
H	1	1	1½	2½	3½	4½	5½

DESIGN OPTIONS

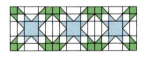

PRECUT FRIENDLY!

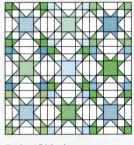

Each 12" block uses:

LC × ⅔ square for A, B

LC × ⅔ square for G, H

YARDAGE FOR LAP QUILT

72" × 72"

12" block

6 × 6 setting = 36 blocks

A, B, G, H: 72 layer cake squares

C, D, E, F: 3½ yards

CUTTING

NOTE *Mix and match sets of 4A/4B and 4G/H to make each block.*

A, B: From each of 36 layer cake squares, cut 4 squares 2½" × 2½" (A) and 4 squares 2⅞" × 2⅞" (B).

G, H: From each of 36 layer cake squares, cut 1 strip 4½"; subcut 1 square 4½" × 4½" (H) and 1 square 2⅞" × 2⅞" (G). Cut 1 strip 2⅞"; subcut 3 squares 2⅞" × 2⅞" (G).

C: Cut 11 strips 2⅞" × WOF; subcut into 144 squares 2⅞" × 2⅞".

D: Cut 9 strips 2½" × WOF; subcut into 144 squares 2½" × 2½".

E: Cut 16 strips 2½" × WOF; subcut into 144 rectangles 2½" × 4½".

F: Cut 5 strips 5¼" × WOF; subcut into 36 squares 5¼" × 5¼".

Stepping Stones 100

8-GRID

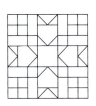
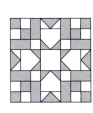
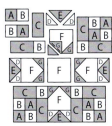
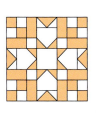

FOR	CUT	NEED	4″	6″	8″	10″	12″
A	8	8	1	1¼	1½	1¾	2
B	12	12	1	1¼	1½	1¾	2
C	8	8	1 × 1½	1¼ × 2	1½ × 2½	1¾ × 3	2 × 3½
D	4	8	1⅜	1⅝	1⅞	2⅛	2⅜
E	1	4	2¼	2¾	3¼	3¾	4¼
F	5	5	1½	2	2½	3	3½
G*	8	8	1	1¼	1½	1¾	2

Refer to Sewing Squares to Squares or Rectangles (page 123)

DESIGN OPTIONS

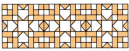
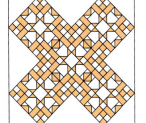

YARDAGE FOR TABLE TOPPER

22½″ × 22½″

8″ block

2 × 2 setting on point = 5 blocks

A, C, E, G: ½ yard

B, D, F, side and corner triangles: ⅝ yard

CUTTING

NOTE *Refer to Side and Corner Triangles for Diagonal Settings (page 127).*

A, G: Cut 3 strips 1½″ × WOF; subcut into 80 squares 1½″ × 1½″ (40A, 40G).

C: Cut 2 strips 1½″ × WOF; subcut into 40 rectangles 1½″ × 2″.

E: Cut 1 strip 3¼″ × WOF; subcut into 5 squares 3¼″ × 3¼″.

B, D, side and corner triangles: Cut 1 strip 12⅝″ × WOF; subcut into 1 square 12⅝″ × 12⅝″ (side triangles), 2 squares 6⅝″ × 6⅝″ (corner triangles), 60 squares 1½″ × 1½″ (B) and 20 squares 1⅞″ × 1⅞″ (D).

F: Cut 2 strips 2½″ × WOF; subcut into 25 squares 2½″ × 2½″.

101 Stockyard's Star

4-GRID

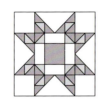

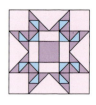

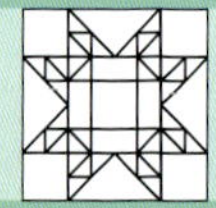

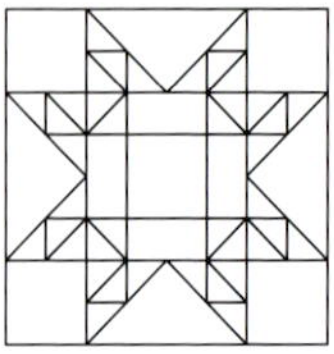

FOR	CUT	NEED	4″	6″	8″	10″	12″
A	4	4	1½	2	2½	3	3½
B	14	28	1⅜	1⅝	1⅞	2⅛	2⅜
C	6	12	1⅜	1⅝	1⅞	2⅛	2⅜
D	1	4	3¼	4¼	5¼	6¼	7¼
E	4	4	1 × 1½	1¼ × 2	1½ × 2½	1¾ × 3	2 × 3½
F	1	1	1½	2	2½	3	3½

DESIGN OPTIONS

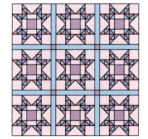

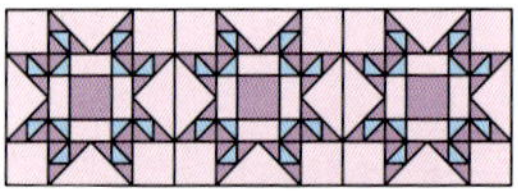

YARDAGE FOR LAP QUILT

64″ × 64″

8″ block

8 × 8 setting = 64 blocks plus sashing and cornerstones

A, D, E: 3⅛ yards

B, F, cornerstones: 2⅔ yards

C, sashing: 2⅛ yards

CUTTING

A: Cut 16 strips 2½″ × WOF; subcut into 256 squares 2½″ × 2½″.

D: Cut 8 strips 5¼″ × WOF; subcut into 64 squares 5¼″ × 5¼″.

E: Cut 16 strips 1½″ × WOF; subcut into 256 rectangles 1½″ × 2½″.

B: Cut 41 strips 1⅞″ × WOF; subcut into 896 squares 1⅞″ × 1⅞″.

F: Cut 4 strips 2½″ × WOF; subcut into 64 squares 2½″ × 2½″.

Cornerstones: Cut 2 strips 1½″ × WOF; subcut into 49 squares 1½″ × 1½″.

C: Cut 18 strips 1⅞″ × WOF; subcut into 384 squares 1⅞″ × 1⅞″.

Sashing: Cut 4 strips 8½″ × WOF; subcut into 112 rectangles 1½″ × 8½″.

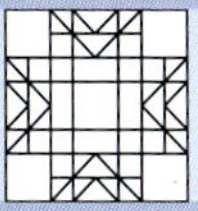

Summer Star 102

 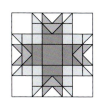 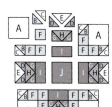 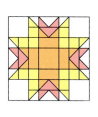

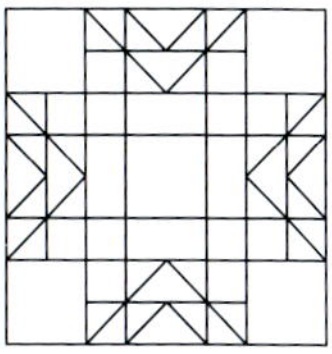

FOR	CUT	NEED	4″	6″	8″	10″	12″
A	4	4	1½	2	2½	3	3½
B	4	8	1⅜	1⅝	1⅞	2⅛	2⅜
C	4	8	1⅜	1⅝	1⅞	2⅛	2⅜
D	4	8	1⅜	1⅝	1⅞	2⅛	2⅜
E	1	4	2¼	2¾	3¼	3¾	4¼
F	12	12	1	1¼	1½	1¾	2
G	4	8	1⅜	1⅝	1⅞	2⅛	2⅜
H	1	4	2¼	2¾	3¼	3¾	4¼
I	4	4	1 × 1½	1¼ × 2	1½ × 2½	1¾ × 3	2 × 3½
J	1	1	1½	2	2½	3	3½

DESIGN OPTIONS

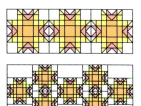

YARDAGE FOR TABLE RUNNER

40″ × 16″

8″ block

7 blocks plus background blocks

A, C, E, background: ⅝ yard

B, F: ⅓ yard

D, H: ¼ yard

G, I, J: ⅓ yard

CUTTING

A, background: Cut 1 strip 8½″ × WOF; subcut into 6 rectangles 4½″ × 8½″ (background) and 12 squares 2½″ × 2½″ (A).

A: Cut 1 strip 2½″ × WOF; subcut into 16 squares 2½″ × 2½″.

C: Cut 2 strips 1⅞″ × WOF; subcut into 28 squares 1⅞″ × 1⅞″.

E: Cut 1 strip 3¼″ × WOF; subcut into 7 squares 3¼″ × 3¼″.

B: Cut 2 strips 1⅞″ × WOF; subcut into 28 squares 1⅞″ × 1⅞″.

F: Cut 3 strips 1½″ × WOF; subcut into 84 squares 1½″ × 1½″.

D: Cut 2 strips 1⅞″ × WOF; subcut into 28 squares 1⅞″ × 1⅞″.

H: Cut 1 strip 3¼″ × WOF; subcut into 7 squares 3¼″ × 3¼″.

G: Cut 2 strips 1⅞″ × WOF; subcut into 28 squares 1⅞″ × 1⅞″.

I: Cut 1 strip 2½″ × WOF; subcut into 28 rectangles 1½″ × 2½″.

J: Cut 1 strip 2½″ × WOF; subcut into 7 squares 2½″ × 2½″.

110 Blocks

103 Sun Ray

3-GRID

 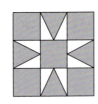 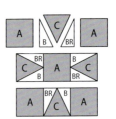

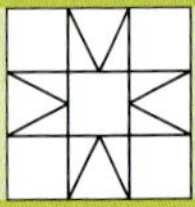

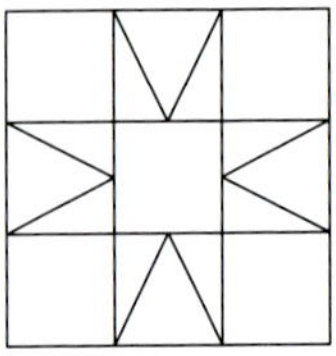

FOR	CUT	NEED	3″	6″	9″	12″	15″
A	5	5	1½	2½	3½	4½	5½
B*	2	4	1½ × 1¾	2¼ × 2½	2¾ × 3½	3¼ × 4½	3¾ × 5½
BR*	2	4	1½ × 1¾	2¼ × 2½	2¾ × 3½	3¼ × 4½	3¾ × 5½
C*	4	4	1½ × 1⅞	2½ × 2⅞	3½ × 3⅞	4½ × 4⅞	5½ × 5⅞

* Refer to Triangle in a Square (page 122).

DESIGN OPTIONS

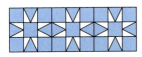

PRECUT FRIENDLY!

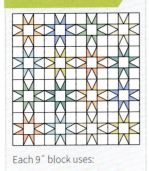

Each 9″ block uses:

FQ × ⅛ for B

YARDAGE FOR TWIN QUILT

63″ × 81″

9″ block

7 × 9 setting = 63 pieced blocks

A, C: 5⅜ yard

B, BR: 8 fat quarters

CUTTING

A: Cut 27 strips 3½″ × WOF; subcut into 315 squares 3½″ × 3½″.

C: Cut 26 strips 3½″ × WOF; subcut into 252 rectangles 3½″ × 3⅞″.

B, BR: From each fat quarter, cut 5 strips 3½″ × WOFQ; subcut into 32 rectangles 2¾″ × 3½″.

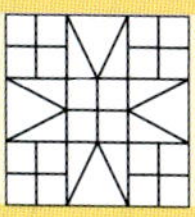

Tennessee Waltz 104

6-GRID

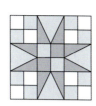
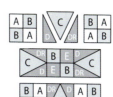
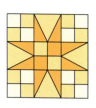

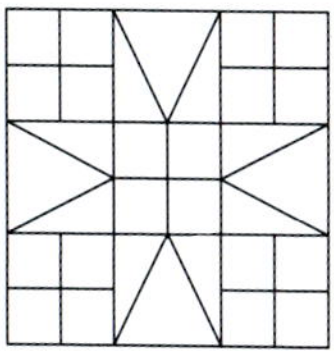

FOR	CUT	NEED	3"	6"	9"	12"	15"
A	8	8	1	1½	2	2½	3
B	10	10	1	1½	2	2½	3
C*	4	4	1½ × 1⅞	2½ × 2⅞	3½ × 3⅞	4½ × 4⅞	5½ × 5⅞
D*	2	4	1½ × 1¾	2¼ × 2½	2¾ × 3½	3¼ × 4½	3¾ × 5½
DR*	2	4	1½ × 1¾	2¼ × 2½	2¾ × 3½	3¼ × 4½	3¾ × 5½
E	2	2	1	1½	2	2½	3

* Refer to Triangle in a Square (page 122).

DESIGN OPTIONS

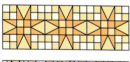

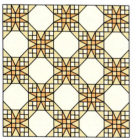

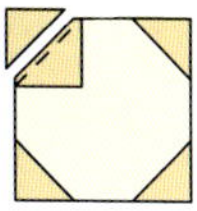

YARDAGE FOR LAP QUILT

60" × 60"

12" block

5 × 5 setting = 25 blocks plus alternate blocks

A, alternate blocks: 2 yards

B, C, alternate block corners: 2⅜ yards

D, DR, E: ⅞ yard

CUTTING

A: Cut 7 strips 2½" × WOF; subcut into 104 squares 2½" × 2½".

Alternate blocks: Cut 4 strips 12½" × WOF; subcut into 12 squares 12½" × 12½".

B: Cut 9 strips 2½" × WOF; subcut into 130 squares 2½" × 2½".

C: Cut 6 strips 4⅞" × WOF; subcut into 52 rectangles 4½" × 4⅞".

Alternate block corners: Cut 6 strips 4½" × WOF; subcut into 48 squares 4½" × 4½".

D, DR: Cut 6 strips 3¼" × WOF; subcut into 52 rectangles 3¼" × 4½".

E: Cut 2 strips 2½" × WOF; subcut into 26 squares 2½" × 2½".

NOTE *Refer to Sewing Squares to Squares or Rectangles (page 123) for alternate block corners.*

105 Trailing Star

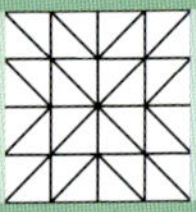

4-GRID

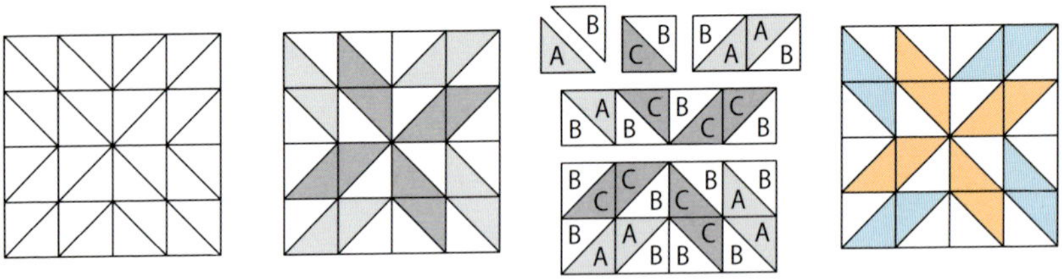

FOR	CUT	NEED	4″	6″	8″	10″	12″
A	4	8	1⅞	2⅜	2⅞	3⅜	3⅞
B	8	16	1⅞	2⅜	2⅞	3⅜	3⅞
C	4	8	1⅞	2⅜	2⅞	3⅜	3⅞

DESIGN OPTIONS

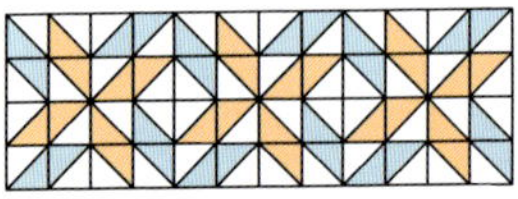

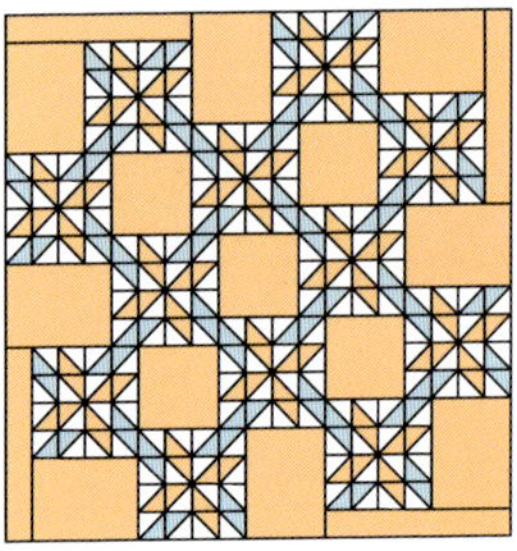

YARDAGE FOR LAP QUILT

57″ × 57″

12″ block

12 blocks with offset setting plus alternate and background blocks

A: ⅝ yard

B: 1¼ yards

C, background: 2 yards

CUTTING

NOTE *Quilt is assembled in sections with partial seams. Sew 9 blocks, then sew the last 3 blocks in the sections as needed. Refer to Sewing Partial Seams (page 123).*

A: Cut 5 strips 3⅞″ × WOF; subcut into 48 squares 3⅞″ × 3⅞″.

B: Cut 10 strips 3⅞″ × WOF; subcut into 96 squares 3⅞″ × 3⅞″.

C: Cut 3 strips 3⅞″ × WOF; subcut into 28 squares 3⅞″ × 3⅞″.

C, background: Cut 4 strips 3⅞″ × WOF; from each strip subcut 5 squares 3⅞″ × 3⅞″ (C) and 1 rectangle 3½″ × 21½″.

Background: Cut 4 strips 9½″ × WOF; subcut into 8 rectangles 9½″ × 12½″ and 5 squares 9½″ × 9½″.

Treasure Star   106

6-GRID

FOR	CUT	NEED	3″	6″	9″	12″	15″
A	2	4	1 3/8	1 7/8	2 3/8	2 7/8	3 3/8
B	6	12	1 3/8	1 7/8	2 3/8	2 7/8	3 3/8
C	6	12	1 3/8	1 7/8	2 3/8	2 7/8	3 3/8
D	2	4	1 3/8	1 7/8	2 3/8	2 7/8	3 3/8
E	1	4	2 1/4	3 1/4	4 1/4	5 1/4	6 1/4
F	2	8	2 1/4	3 1/4	4 1/4	5 1/4	6 1/4
G	1	1	1 7/8	3 3/8	4 3/4	6 1/8	7 5/8

DESIGN OPTIONS

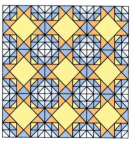

YARDAGE FOR LAP QUILT

72″ × 72″

12″ block

6 × 6 setting = 36 blocks

A: 5/8 yard

B: 1 1/2 yards

C, E: 2 1/4 yards

D, G: 1 3/4 yards

F: 1 1/2 yards

CUTTING

A: Cut 6 strips 2 7/8″ × WOF; subcut into 72 squares 2 7/8″ × 2 7/8″.

B: Cut 16 strips 2 7/8″ × WOF; subcut into 216 squares 2 7/8″ × 2 7/8″.

C: Cut 16 strips 2 7/8″ × WOF; subcut into 216 squares 2 7/8″ × 2 7/8″.

E: Cut 5 strips 5 1/4″ × WOF; subcut into 36 squares 5 1/4″ × 5 1/4″.

D: Cut 6 strips 2 7/8″ × WOF; subcut into 72 squares 2 7/8″ × 2 7/8″.

G: Cut 6 strips 6 1/8″ × WOF; subcut into 36 squares 6 1/8″ × 6 1/8″.

F: Cut 9 strips 5 1/4″ × WOF; subcut into 72 squares 5 1/4″ × 5 1/4″.

110 Blocks

107 Union Star

 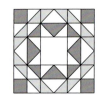 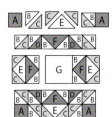 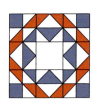

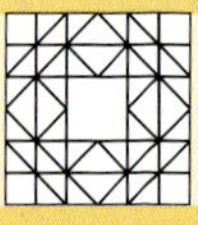

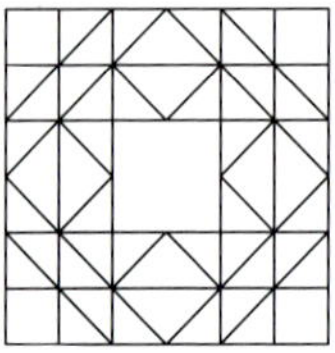

FOR	CUT	NEED	3″	6″	9″	12″	15″
A	4	4	1	1½	2	2½	3
B	10	20	1⅜	1⅞	2⅜	2⅞	3⅜
C	8	16	1⅜	1⅞	2⅜	2⅞	3⅜
D	2	4	1⅜	1⅞	2⅜	2⅞	3⅜
E	1	4	2¼	3¼	4¼	5¼	6¼
F	1	4	2¼	3¼	4¼	5¼	6¼
G	1	1	1½	2½	3½	4½	5½

DESIGN OPTIONS

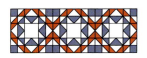
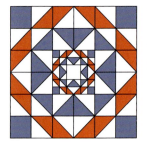

YARDAGE FOR WALL HANGING

36″ × 36″

12″ and 36″ blocks

2 blocks

A, D, F: ½ yard

B, E, G: ¾ yard

C: ⅝ yard

CUTTING

NOTE *Each E and F triangle in the 36″ block are made with 2 half-square triangles.*

A (12″, 36″), D (12″), F (12″): Cut 1 strip 6½″ × WOF; subcut into 4 squares 6½″ × 6½″ (A-36″), 1 square 5¼″ × 5¼″ (F), 2 squares 2⅞″ × 2⅞″ (D), and 4 squares 2½″ × 2½″ (A-12″).

D (36″), F (36″ HST): Cut 1 strip 6⅞″ × WOF; subcut into 6 squares 6⅞″ × 6⅞″ (2D, 4F).

B (12″, 36″), E (12″, 36″ HST), G (12″): Cut 3 strips 6⅞″ × WOF; subcut into 14 squares 6⅞″ × 6⅞″ (10B-36″, 4E-36″), 1 square 5¼″ × 5¼″ (E-12″), 1 square 4½″ × 4½″ (G), 10 squares 2⅞″ × 2⅞″ (B-12″).

C (12″, 36″): Cut 2 strips 6⅞″ × WOF; subcut into 8 squares 6⅞″ × 6⅞″ (36″), 8 squares 2⅞″ × 2⅞″ (12″).

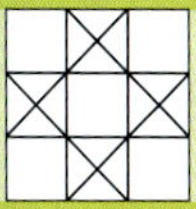

3-GRID

Variable Star 108

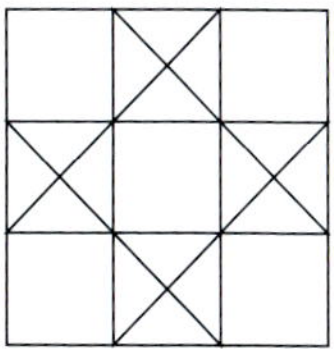

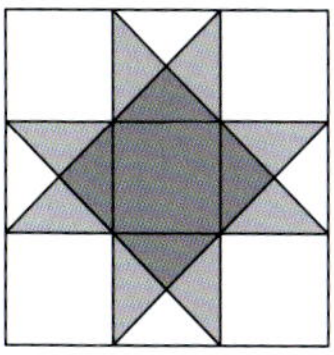

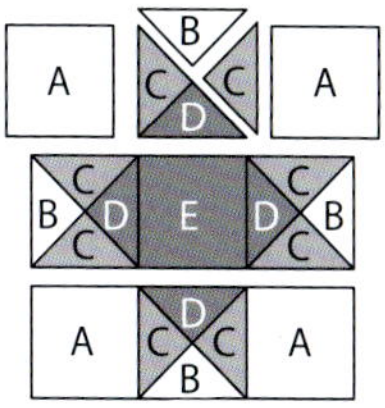

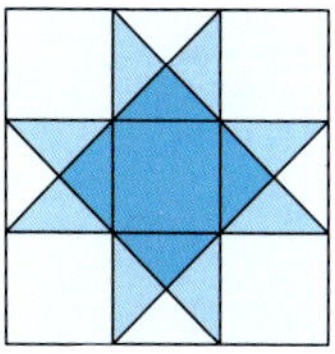

FOR	CUT	NEED	3″	6″	9″	12″	15″
A	4 ☐	4 ☐	1½	2½	3½	4½	5½
B	1 ☐	4 ⊠	2¼	3¼	4¼	5¼	6¼
C	2 ☐	8 ⊠	2¼	3¼	4¼	5¼	6¼
D	1 ☐	4 ⊠	2¼	3¼	4¼	5¼	6¼
E	1 ☐	1 ☐	1½	2½	3½	4½	5½

DESIGN OPTIONS

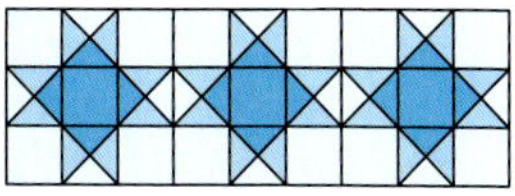

PRECUT FRIENDLY!

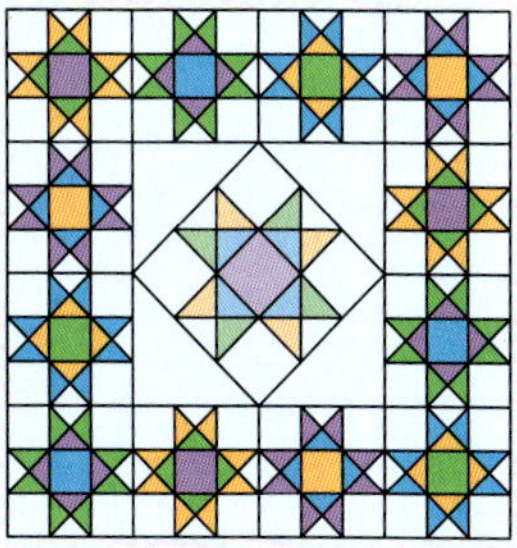

Each 12″ block uses:

FQ × ⅔ fat quarter for C

FQ × ⅙ fat quarter for D

FQ × ⅙ fat quarter for E

YARDAGE FOR BABY QUILT

48″ × 48″

12″ and 17″ blocks

12 × 12″ + 1 × 17″ = 13 blocks plus corner triangles

A, B, corner triangles: 1⅞ yards

C, D, E: 5 fat quarters

CUTTING

NOTE *Refer to Side and Corner Triangles for Diagonal Settings (page 127). The C triangles are 2 colors in the 17″ block. Mix and match sets of 1B, 2C, and 1D for the 12″ blocks.*

A, 12″: Cut 6 strips 4½″ × WOF; subcut into 48 squares 4½″ × 4½″.

A, 17″: Cut 1 strip 6⅛″ × WOF; subcut into 4 squares 6⅛″ × 6⅛″.

B, 12″: Cut 2 strips 5¼″ × WOF; subcut into 12 squares 5¼″ × 5¼″.

B (17″), corner triangles: Cut 1 strip 12⅞″ × WOF; subcut into 2 squares 12⅞″ × 12⅞″ (corner triangles) and 1 square 6⅞″ × 6⅞″ (B).

From each of 3 fat quarters: Cut 1 square 6⅞″ × 6⅞″ (C/D-17″), 3 squares 4½″ × 4½″ (E-12″) and 8 squares 5¼″ × 5¼″ (C/D-12″).

From 1 fat quarter: Cut 1 square 6⅛″ × 6⅛″ (E-17″), 3 squares 4½″ × 4½″ (E-12″) and 6 squares 5¼″ × 5¼″ (C/D-12″).

From 1 fat quarter: Cut 6 squares 5¼″ × 5¼″ (C/D-12″).

109 Wandering Star

3-GRID

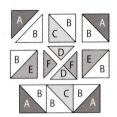
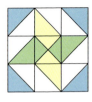

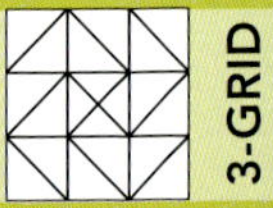

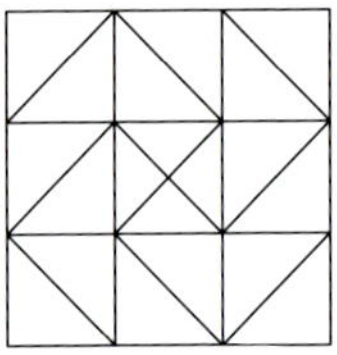

FOR	CUT	NEED	3″	6″	9″	12″	15″
A	2	4	1⅞	2⅞	3⅞	4⅞	5⅞
B	4	8	1⅞	2⅞	3⅞	4⅞	5⅞
C	1	2	1⅞	2⅞	3⅞	4⅞	5⅞
D	1	2	2¼	3¼	4¼	5¼	6¼
E	1	2	1⅞	2⅞	3⅞	4⅞	5⅞
F	1	2	2¼	3¼	4¼	5¼	6¼

DESIGN OPTIONS

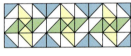
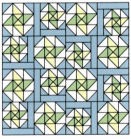

YARDAGE FOR LAP QUILT

60″ × 60″

12″ and 15″ blocks

4 × 4 setting = 16 blocks

A, sashing: 1½ yards

B: 1⅝ yards

C, D: ⅞ yard

E, F: ⅞ yard

CUTTING

A, 12″: Cut 2 strips 4⅞″ × WOF; subcut into 16 squares 4⅞″ × 4⅞″.

A, 15″: Cut 3 strips 5⅞″ × WOF; subcut into 16 squares 5⅞″ × 5⅞″.

Sashing: Cut 6 strips 3½″ × WOF; subcut each of 4 strips into 1 rectangle 3½″ × 15½″ and 2 rectangles 3½″ × 12½″, and the last 2 strips into 4 rectangles 3½″ × 15½″.

B, 12″: Cut 4 strips 4⅞″ × WOF; subcut into 32 squares 4⅞″ × 4⅞″.

B, 15″: Cut 5 strips 5⅞″ × WOF; subcut into 32 squares 5⅞″ × 5⅞″.

C, 12″: Cut 1 strip 4⅞″ × WOF; subcut into 8 squares 4⅞″ × 4⅞″.

C, 15″: Cut 1 strip 5⅞″ × WOF; subcut into 7 squares 5⅞″ × 5⅞″.

D, 12″: Cut 1 strip 5¼″ × WOF; subcut into 4 squares 5¼″ × 5¼″.

C (15″), D (15″): Cut 1 strip 6¼″ × WOF; subcut into 4 squares 6¼″ × 6¼″ (D) and 1 square 5⅞″ × 5⅞″ (C).

E, 12″: Cut 1 strip 4⅞″ × WOF; subcut into 8 squares 4⅞″ × 4⅞″.

E, 15″: Cut 1 strip 5⅞″ × WOF; subcut into 7 squares 5⅞″ × 5⅞″.

F, 12″: Cut 1 strip 5¼″ × WOF; subcut into 4 squares 5¼″ × 5¼″.

E (15″), F (15″): Cut 1 strip 6¼″ × WOF; subcut into 4 squares 6¼″ × 6¼″ (F) and 1 square 5⅞″ × 5⅞″ (E).

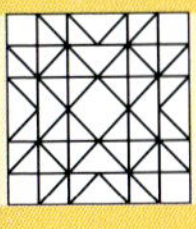

Wyoming Valley — 110

6-GRID

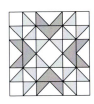
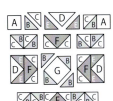
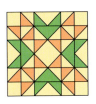

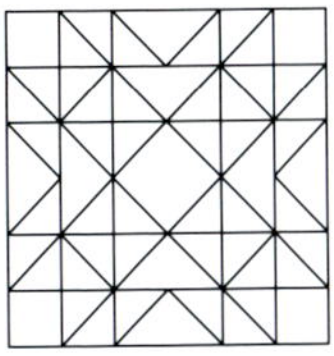

FOR	CUT	NEED	3″	6″	9″	12″	15″
A	4	4	1	1½	2	2½	3
B	8	16	1⅜	1⅞	2⅜	2⅞	3⅜
C	10	20	1⅜	1⅞	2⅜	2⅞	3⅜
D	1	4	2¼	3¼	4¼	5¼	6¼
E	4	8	1⅜	1⅞	2⅜	2⅞	3⅜
F	1	4	2¼	3¼	4¼	5¼	6¼
G	1	1	1¼	1⅞	2⅝	3⅜	4

DESIGN OPTIONS

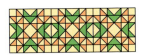

PRECUT FRIENDLY!

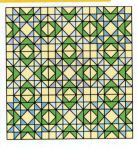

Each 9″ block uses:

Jelly roll × ½ strip for B

YARDAGE BABY QUILT

54″ × 54″

9″ block

6 × 6 setting = 36 blocks

A, C, D, G: 2¾ yards

B: 18 jelly roll strips

E, F: 1¼ yards

CUTTING

A: Cut 7 strips 2″ × WOF; subcut into 144 squares 2″ × 2″.

C: Cut 22 strips 2⅜″ × WOF; subcut into 360 squares 2⅜″ × 2⅜″.

D: Cut 4 strips 4¼″ × WOF; subcut into 36 squares 4¼″ × 4¼″.

G: Cut 3 strips 2⅝″ × WOF; subcut into 36 squares 2⅝″ × 2⅝″.

B: Trim each jelly roll strip to 16 squares 2⅜″ × 2⅜″.

E: Cut 9 strips 2⅜″ × WOF; subcut into 144 squares 2⅜″ × 2⅜″.

F: Cut 4 strips 4¼″ × WOF; subcut into 36 squares 4¼″ × 4¼″.

Tips and Helpful Charts

TRIANGLE IN A SQUARE
Cutting Center Triangle

1. Place the center rectangle with the longer sides horizontal.

2. Measure along the top edge from each upper corner and mark the measurement noted in the Trim from Corner column of the chart.

3. Cut the triangle from the lower corner to the upper mark on each side.

Cutting Side Triangles

1. Place 2 side rectangles right sides together with the shorter sides horizontal.

There are 2 exceptions: The rectangles for the 1″ finished TNS block are cut with the **longer** sides horizontal, and the side triangles for the 1½″ finished TNS block are cut from squares.

2. Measure from the upper left corner along the top edge and mark ½″ from the corner. Repeat for the lower right corner, measuring along the bottom edge.

3. Cut the side triangles diagonally from the lower mark to the upper mark. This creates 2 sets of triangles.

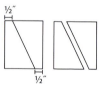

FINISHED BLOCK SIZE	CENTER CUT SIZE	TRIM FROM CORNER	SIDE CUT SIZE (CUT 2)
1″	1⅞″ × 1½″	¾″	1¾″ × 1½″
1½″	2⅜″ × 2″	1″	2″ × 2″
2″	2⅞″ × 2½″	1¼″	2¼″ × 2½″
2½″	3⅜″ × 3″	1½″	2½″ × 3″
3″	3⅞″ × 3½″	1¾″	2¾″ × 3½″
4″	4⅞″ × 4½″	2¼″	3¼″ × 4½″
5″	5⅞″ × 5½″	2¾″	3¾″ × 5½″

Sewing Triangle in a Square

1. Match a left side triangle along the left edge of the center triangle and stitch. Press and trim off the dog-ears.

2. Repeat Step 1 with a right side triangle along the right edge.

3. If needed, trim ¼" beyond the triangle points to a square that is ½" larger than the finished size.

MIX AND MATCH BLOCKS

Design exciting new quilts by mixing various blocks in different combinations. For the most successful designs, combine 2-, 4-, 8-grid blocks; 3-, 6-, and 9-grid blocks; or 2- and 6- grid blocks. The seams in these similar grids line up nicely both visually and for easy stitching.

SEWING SQUARES TO SQUARES OR RECTANGLES

1. Place the square at the corner of the larger square or rectangle, right sides together.

2. Sew diagonally from corner to corner.

3. Trim and press.

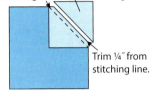

SEWING PARTIAL SEAMS

1. Place the first pieced unit or strip on one edge of the center square/ unit. Beginning ½" in from the edge of the center square/ unit, stitch along the top edge.

2. Working clockwise around the center a square/unit, stitch the second pieced unit/strip. Repeat for the remaining two pieced units/strips.

3. Finish stitching the first pieced unit/strip. Press.

Red = Completed stitches.

CORNER ALIGNMENT FOR PIECING SHAPES

First five sets are courtesy of Alex Anderson; reprinted from *Simply Stars*.

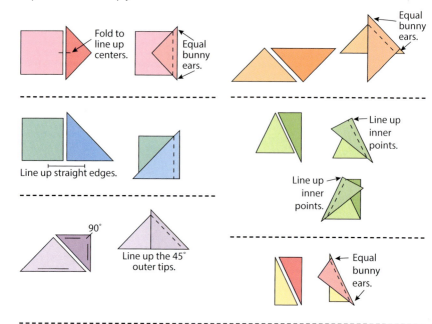

YARDAGE FOR SQUARES

Cut size	¼ yd.	½ yd.	¾ yd.	1 yd.
1½″	168	336	504	672
2″	84	189	273	378
2½″	48	112	160	224
3″	42	84	126	168
3½″	24	60	84	120
4″	20	40	60	90
4½″	18	36	54	72
5″	8	24	40	56
5½″	7	21	28	42
6″	7	21	28	42
6½″	6	12	24	30
7″	6	12	18	30
7½″	5	10	15	20
	5	10	15	20
8½″	4	8	12	16
9″	4	8	12	16
9½″		4	8	12
10″		4	8	12
10½″		4	8	12
11″		3	6	9
11½″		3	6	9
12″		3	6	9
12½″		3	6	6
13″		3	6	6

STANDARD MATTRESS SIZES

Crib: 27″ × 52″

Twin: 39″ × 75″

Twin Long: 39″ × 80″

Double: 54″ × 75″

Double Long: 54″ × 80″

Queen: 60″ × 80″

King: 76″ × 80″

Cal King: 72″ × 84″

King Dual: 78″ × 80″

YARDAGE FOR RECTANGLES

Cut size	½ yd.	¾ yd.	1 yd.
1″ × 1½″	504	756	1008
1 × 2	378	567	756
1 × 2½	288	432	576
1 × 2⅞	252	378	504
1⅛ × 3⅜	192	288	384
1¼ × 2¾	210	315	420
1¼ × 3⅞	140	210	280
1⅜ × 4⅛	130	190	260
1½ × 1⅞	264	396	528
1½ × 2½	192	288	384
1½ × 2¾	180	270	360
1½ × 3½	144	216	288
1½ × 4½	108	162	216
1⅝ × 4⅞	88	128	176
1¾ × 3	140	210	280
1¾ × 3¼	120	180	240
1¾ × 5⅞	70	105	140
1⅞ × 5⅝	63	98	133
2 × 3½	108	156	216
2 × 5	72	104	144
2 × 6⅞	54	78	108
2¼ × 2½	128	192	256
2¼ × 4¼	72	108	144
2½ × 3	98	140	196
2½ × 4½	63	90	126
2½ × 8½	28	40	56
2¾ × 3½	72	108	156
2¾ × 5¼	48	72	104
3 × 5½	42	63	84
3 × 10½	24	36	48
3¼ × 4½	45	72	99
3¼ × 6¼	30	48	66
3½ × 3⅞	50	70	100
3½ × 6½	30	42	60
3¾ × 7¼	20	35	45
4½ × 4⅞	32	48	64
5½ × 5⅞	21	28	42

FIGURING FABRIC FOR A QUILT

To determine how much of each fabric you'll need for the blocks in a quilt:

1. Choose a block (or blocks) you want to use.

2. Determine how many blocks you'll need to create a quilt in the desired size.

3. Figure how many of each size square and rectangle you'll need from each fabric and refer to Yardage for Squares (page 124) and Yardage for Rectangles at left.

It's as easy as that!

DIAGONAL MEASUREMENTS OF BLOCKS

Block Size	Width on Point
3″	4¼″
4″	5⅝″
4½″	6⅜″
5″	7 1/16″
6″	8½″
7½″	10⅝″
8″	11 5/16″
9″	12¾″
10″	14⅛″
12″	17″
12½″	17 11/16″
13½″	19 1/16″
15″	21¼″
18″	25 7/16″
22½″	31 13/16″

Tips and Helpful Charts

SEWING HALF-SQUARE TRIANGLES

1. With right sides together, pair 2 squares. Lightly draw a diagonal line from one corner to the opposite corner on the wrong sides of one square. (Fig. A)

2. Sew a scant ¼″ seam on each side of the line. (Fig. B)

3. Cut on the drawn line. (Fig. C)

4. Press, and trim off the dog ears. (Fig. D)

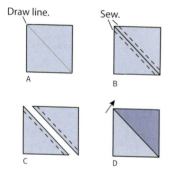

SEWING FLYING GEESE WITH TRIANGLES

1. Place a small triangle right sides together with the large triangle, matching the lower 45° corners. The small triangle will extend past the center of the large triangle.

2. Sew the triangles together with a ¼″ seam. Press the seam open and trim off the dog-ears.

3. Repeat Step 1 with the second small triangle on the other side of the large triangle.

4. The seams should cross the point of the large triangle ¼″ from the top edge.

EASY-CUT 45° ANGLES

Place the 45° line of the ruler on the edge of the fabric and trim as shown. Rotate the ruler and repeat if needed.

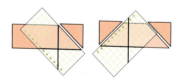

SIDE AND CORNER TRIANGLES FOR DIAGONAL SETTINGS

Finished Block Size	Cut Squares for Side Triangles*	Cut Squares for Corner Triangles**
3"	5½"	3"
4"	7"	3¾"
5"	8⅜"	4½"
6"	9¾"	5⅛"
7½"	11⅞"	6¼"
8"	12⅝"	6⅝"
9"	14"	7¼"
10"	15⅜"	8"
12"	18¼"	9⅜"
12½"	19"	9¾"
15"	22½"	11½"
18"	26¾"	13⅝"

* Cut in half diagonally, twice
** Cut in half diagonally

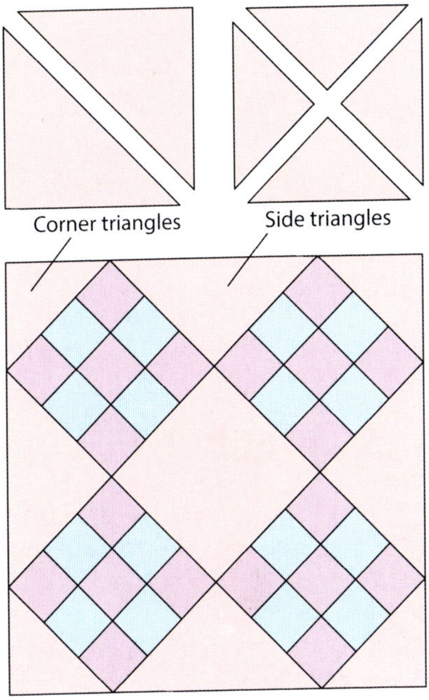

About the Author

Photo by Nick Riley Photography

Debbie Rodgers is the Senior Technical Editor at C&T Publishing. She's always working on at least five sewing, quilting, or knitting projects, with other thread and yarn crafts also in rotation. Debbie and her very patient husband live in Northern California, where he, her brothers, and two nephews built her an amazing light-filled sewing studio.

CREATIVE SPARK
ONLINE LEARNING

Quilting courses to become an expert quilter...

From their studio to yours, Creative Spark instructors are teaching you how to create and become a master of your craft. So not only do you get a look inside their creative space, you also get to be a part of engaging courses that would typically be a one or multi-day workshop from the comfort of your home.

Creative Spark is not your one-size-fits-all online learning experience. We welcome you to be who you are, share, create, and belong.

Scan for a gift from us

creativespark.ctpub.com